A Translation, History,
and Commentary
by William F. Hansen

Saxo Grammaticus & the

LIFE OF HAMLET

University of Nebraska Press
Lincoln and London
1983

The paper is this book
meets the guidelines
for permanence and
durability of the
Committee on Production
Guidelines for Book
Longevity of the Council
on Library Resources.

Library of Congress
Cataloging in
Publication Data

Saxo Grammaticus, d. ca. 1204.
Saxo Grammaticus and
the Life of Hamlet.

Translation of:
Gesta Danorum.
Liber 3, VI-4, II.
Bibliography: p.
Includes Index.
1. Hamlet - Legends.
2. Shakespeare, William,
1564-1616.
Hamlet - Sources.
I. Hansen, William F., 1941-
II. Title
PR2807.A77E5 1983
948.9'01 82-2671
AACR2
ISBN 0-8032-2318-8

To
my mother
and
father

Contents

Illustrations

Preface

Once a living story that circulated orally in the North, the legend of Hamlet is now known only from the written texts that it inspired. Of these, Saxo's account of Hamlet has a special interest, in addition to its intrinsic value as a good story, for it is the earliest known narrative of the hero's life as well as the ultimate source of Shakespeare's play. In the present book I present a fresh translation of Saxo's narrative, and I explore the Hamlet story as an oral story, Saxo's text as a literary text, and the relationship between the two.

The Introduction is essentially a brief history of the Hamlet story from the first evidence to Shakespeare. We do not have access to Saxo's own sources; indeed, we do not know who or what they were. So I begin with a survey of what we do know about the Hamlet of tradition before and after Saxo, and from it I try to judge how freely or conservatively Saxo has treated the events of the oral story. Then I turn to what might be called the prehistory of the Hamlet story. By comparing Hamlet with similar traditional heroes I try to determine whether the story of the cunning Dane who played the fool is entirely isolated and unique or is genetically related to other legends and therefore part of a larger tradition. For if Hamlet has relatives, their history is part of his history. I do not, however, take up the old problem of the origin of the Hamlet story, not because the question is uninteresting, but because it appears to be unanswerable.

Two important forces competed for Saxo's favor when he was retelling the story: the oral and the written traditions, each having in some measure its own way of telling a tale. So I examine how—and to what extent—Saxo has transformed the oral legend into a literary text. Finally, I turn from medieval Denmark to Renaissance England and observe how Hamlet, now a literary figure, was refashioned by English playwrights for the Elizabethan stage.

Accuracy of sense and clarity of expression were my principal, if also elusive, ideals in rendering Saxo's *Life of Hamlet* into English. I have not wished to give the translation an especially Latinate or archaic flavor (though a particular few archaisms seemed handier to use than to shun), but at the same time I wanted to maintain the formal tone. The result, I think, is much more modern than Oliver Elton's translation from 1893 and somewhat less colloquial than Peter Fisher's from 1979. The Latin text is that of Jørgen Olrik and Hans Ræder.

Although Saxo's narrative does not require a commentary in order to be read with pleasure, many features of the story are confusing or lost to the present-day reader who comes to the tale without any aid. A reader unacquainted with Old Scandinavian literature and culture is not likely to know the nature of Danish wall hangings or sworn brotherhood or funerals or other matters with which Saxo assumes his thirteenth-century readers to be familiar. Even one who comes to the narrative well acquainted with the cultural background must inevitably miss many of the plays on words and other subtleties such as the meaning of the message carried by the gadfly or of the hero's bed of flowers in the fen, since most of these things cannot be extracted directly from Saxo's text or a translation of it, but nevertheless are implied by the narrative. Finally, a reader is likely to puzzle over certain difficult scenes and perhaps fail to perceive that the fault lies, not in the reading, but in the storytelling. All these matters are the subject of the Commentary. The treatment is inevitably fuller than that of Hilda Ellis Davidson and Peter Fisher, whose commentary on Saxo covers the first nine books of Saxo's work. There is, however, much that I do not comment upon: this is not intended to be a philological commentary or a catalogue of parallels. If I judged that a comment would not illuminate or at least identify an obscurity, or make implicit meanings explicit, I did not add one.

The other early Danish accounts of Hamlet are translated and discussed at the end of the study, in Appendix I. These little texts probably have not been translated before into a modern language. Appendix II briefly deals with the first Hamlet illustrations.

I have received much help in making this book. I am especially indebted to Joseph Fontenrose and W. Edson Richmond, both of whom read my manuscript through at one stage or another and offered many useful suggestions for improvement; to Bengt Holbek, my folkloristic interlocutor in Denmark; to Iver Kjær, who checked my renderings of early Danish; to Niels Lukman, who permitted me to read his unpublished manuscript on Amleth and Hamlet; and to my wife, Marcia Cebulska, whose enthusiasm and good ideas were welcome ingredients.

I am also grateful for the help or inspiration of William Aspinall, Charles Forker, Judith Friedman-Hansen, Henry Glassie, James Halporn, Thomas Jacobsen, Marie K. Jensen, Thorkild and Aase Jensen, George Koniaris, Stanley Kozial, Egon and Grethe Malm, Asta Nielsen, Arthur Stabler, Ian Thomson, and Cecil Wooten.

To the Royal Library, Copenhagen, and the Royal Library, Stockholm, I am indebted for permission to reproduce the photographs that appear as figures 1–4 in this book.

And finally I am happy to express my thanks to the University of California, Berkeley, for the Amy Bowles Johnson Memorial Traveling Fellowship in Classics (1968/69), which enabled me as a graduate student to begin research in Denmark on the Hamlet story; to the American-Scandinavian Foundation for an Honorary Fellowship (1968/69); to the National Endowment of the Humanities for the grant of a Younger Humanist Fellowship

(1972/73), which allowed me to return to Denmark once again; and to Indiana University, Bloomington, for several research fellowships and grants.

Translator's Introduction

One: The Hamlet Story

Saxo was the first person, so far as anyone knows, to compose a *Life of Hamlet*. The little biography is found in his *Gesta Danorum*, or *History of the Danes*, which he composed in Latin in the years around 1200. In its sixteen books Saxo traces the Danes from their eponymous ancestor Dan to his own times.[1] The story of Amleth, as Saxo calls him, is related at the end of book 3 and the beginning of book 4, during the reigns of Rørik and of Viglek, in the distant past, well before the Christian era.

According to Saxo, King Rørik of Denmark put the brothers Ørvendil and Fengi in charge of Jutland. Ørvendil won the hand of the king's daughter Geruth, by whom he had a son Amleth. But Fengi was envious of his brother, murdered him, wed his widow, and ruled Jutland alone. Fearing for his life, Amleth played the fool. Fengi, however, was not entirely convinced of his nephew's folly, and tested him by bringing him together with a fair maiden in the woods. For if Amleth was sane, Fengi thought, he would have sexual relations with the girl. But Amleth eluded the trap. The king next arranged for an eavesdropper to conceal himself in Geruth's room to overhear the conversation of the queen and her son, but Amleth foiled this trap also. Fengi now decided that his nephew should be killed. The king sent him with two escorts and a fatal letter to the king of Britain, but Amleth rewrote Fengi's letter, instructing the British king to execute Amleth's escorts instead and to give his daughter in marriage to Amleth. Returning to Denmark just as men were celebrating his funeral, Amleth joined in the celebration as cup-bearer, encouraging the men to be merry and to drink deeply. When they were drunkenly sleeping, he put into effect an extraordinary plan of revenge. On the following day the Jutes acclaimed him king. Not only did Amleth exact his vengeance and live, but he also had further adventures. After Amleth went back to Britain, the king, his father-in-law, tried to arrange for his death by dispatching him to sue on the king's behalf for the hand of the queen of Scotland. It was her grim practice to slay her suitors. But Amleth himself married her and later overcame the British monarch and his men. He returned with his two wives to Denmark, where eventually he fell in battle against King Rørik's successor, Viglek.

The Life of Hamlet as Oral Legend

We have no reason to believe that Amleth is a historical character or that any of the events that Saxo relates in his *Vita Amlethi* (as I shall call it) ever happened, either in the pre-Christian period or later. At least there is no evidence to support a belief that Amleth has existed anywhere other than in story. We can ask, then, where the historian got his tale. Did he make it up himself, or is it a traditional narrative that once circulated orally in Denmark?

We can set aside the possibility that the *Vita* is fiction created by Saxo and passed off by him as early Danish history. For one thing, there are features of the story that Saxo records but certainly misunderstands. When, for example, Amleth tells his uncle's men that he lay on an animal's hoof, a cock's comb, and some roof beams, Saxo fails to perceive that Amleth is punning, and so interprets Amleth's statement literally, with mildly absurd results (sec.4).[2] If Saxo misses the point of the scene, he is not likely to have created it. And since the puns are Danish, it is obvious that whoever first devised the scene intended it to be communicated in Danish rather than in Latin. When, moreover, Saxo gives two different versions of a motif in the episode of the British king's feast (sec.6), we can infer that he had more than one source or informant, at least for this episode. It seems in fact very likely that Saxo drew upon a variety of sources, for part of the story is thick with Danish puns (sec. 4), whereas Undensakre, the mysterious place that Saxo says is unknown to his people, is almost certainly an Icelandic term that the Danish historian has transmitted but not understood (sec. 10). In short, all the evidence indicates that the *Vita Amlethi* is, not literary fiction, but a literary retelling of an oral legend. Later we shall see that Saxo's story has analogues in European traditional story.

Now, it is known that Saxo, in assembling heroic legends for his *Gesta Danorum*, drew not only on contemporary Danish tradition but also on West Scandinavian tradition, the latter including principally the lore of Iceland and Norway. If a particular story in Saxo's work shows linguistic forms or narrative motifs or stylistic features which are closer to, say, Icelandic than to Danish practice, it is reasonable to infer that the tale derives from Icelandic rather than from Danish tradition. That is not to say that the story necessarily was found exclusively in Iceland or even only among the West Scandinavians, but that Saxo's immediate source or sources for it were, if not actually Icelandic, then at least not far removed from Icelandic oral storytelling. From around the mid-thirteenth century onwards these oral stories also received literary treatment in Iceland as *fornaldarsögur* (that is, "sagas of ancient times"). The sagas recount the adventures of heroes who were imagined to have lived in a period before the settlement of Iceland, which began around A.D. 870. Some stories are common to the *Gesta Danorum* and a *fornaldarsaga*, while others are known only from the one or the other.[3]

Probably Saxo's story is for the most part native, that is, a story told largely as it was known from Danish oral tradition. The action is, after all, localized in Denmark, the hero is a Dane, and his name appears in a Jutish (that is, West Danish) form. Moreover, the storytelling style is not characteristically Icelandic, for it is hard to imagine that Icelandic narrators, with their fondness for names, would not have names for such characters as the hero's foster siblings, Fengi's eavesdropping friend, the two henchmen who escort Amleth to Britain, or the king of Britain himself.[4] Probably the simplest interpretation of the evidence is that Saxo has enlarged a native Jutish account of the hero with features of the story as it was known to the Icelanders. This explanation would be in harmony with Saxo's manifest eagerness to include everything connected with the Hamlet tradition, even when it is artistically extraneous (for example, the variant motif cited above) or is of no obvious importance (for example, the obscure fate of the even more obscure Fjaller in sec. 10) or cannot be rendered into Latin (the Scandinavian wordplay). If this is correct, the *Vita Amlethi* is a literary treatment of a traditional oral story (whether Saxo's own immediate sources were oral or, less likely, written), though of the story in a collated form such as it never had in a single region's storytelling tradition.

Since most of the evidence for the Hamlet legend in Denmark rests with Saxo's account, it is difficult to judge how freely he himself has handled the story. Indeed, it is no doubt an oversimplification to speak of *the story*, as though it necessarily had in medieval Denmark a single, unchanging form. For it is, of course, the usual case with oral narratives that at one time there can be heard longer and shorter versions, fine tellings and poor, variations reflecting personal or class or regional or ethnic interests, and so on. Jutes and Zealanders probably told the tale somewhat differently, as aristocrats and thralls must have done, if the hero once was generally known throughout the land and among the various levels of society.[5] It seems likely, as I have suggested, that Saxo did actively seek out as much information concerning the hero's life as he could find, drawing on both Danish and Icelandic traditions, so that his *Vita Amlethi* rests on a deliberate collation of information coming from more than one place. In addition, he obviously deviated from local practice when he narrated the tale, not in his native tongue, but in the learned and international language of his day. But did he also modify in any important way the traditional plot of the story?

The slight evidence that we have suggests that Saxo did change some details. There is a brief account of Hamlet in *The Annals of Ryd*, a Jutish composition dating to the middle of the thirteenth century, one of five early Danish annals and chronicles that mention the hero (see Appendix I). According to *The Annals of Ryd*, Amblet (as he is there called) and his father and his uncle were national monarchs, that is, kings of Denmark and not only of Jutland. But Saxo, whose bias for Zealand suggests that he himself was a Zealander, not only presents them as regional kings but even describes the founder of the line as a mere jarl. If this is not simply the Zealandic way of telling the legend, it must be the result of Saxo's manipulations of the story (Commentary, sec. 1). Saxo and the compiler of *The Annals of Ryd* also disagree about the site of Hamlet's death, and it appears likely that Saxo has replaced the traditional location with one of his own (Commentary, sec. 10). Although none of these details is very weighty in itself, Saxo's innovations (if this is what they are) indicate that he did not look upon the Hamlet story as a sacred trust that he should transmit entirely without change to his readers. Beyond this, it appears, we can only speculate.

The Hamlet Story in Iceland

We must also make do with uncertainties when we inquire about the Icelandic tradition upon which the Dane drew, since no information concerning an Icelandic Hamlet from Saxo's own time has been preserved. About two centuries before Saxo, however, an Icelandic poet refers to sand as "Amloði's meal," and it is all but certain that he is alluding to a little event that is known to us more fully in Saxo's *Vita Amlethi* (Commentary, sec. 4). In the latter, the king's men once tell Amleth that the white sandhills they have come upon are really piles of flour, and Amleth agrees, saying that it has been ground and bleached by the storms of the sea. What is interesting is, not that Saxo may have learned this incident from an Icelander, but that around the year 1000 the incident was familiar enough to Icelanders that they could catch an allusion to it. If there was a well-known anecdote about Amloði, there probably was a larger, connected story about him. But if there was, we know nothing further about it.

Amlóði is the Icelandic form of the hero's name, corresponding to what in Danish accounts is given variously as *Amblothæ, Amblupe, Amlæd, Amblet, Amleth,* and so on. As a common noun *amlóði* is current in Icelandic in the sense of "an imbecile, weak person," and it survives in Norwegian dialect as *amlod* 'a fool'. In Swedish it appears once, either as a name or as a common noun, in a poetic chronicle of the early fourteenth century.[6]

Then the king clapped his hands
And laughed heartily and made merry
Just as though he were an *amblodhe*
Who was not in his right mind.[7]

So the word or name is found throughout Scandinavia. There have been attempts to find for it an etymology that accords with the apparent nature of the hero as a fool, although the etymologists have on the whole shown little agreement.[8] It has otherwise been conjectured that the name received its meaning from the story itself and passed therefrom into speech as a common noun. In other words, the hero was given his name not because he played the fool, but because he did so, his name came to bear that meaning. There is, however, no other instance from Germanic legend in which the name of a hero has passed into speech as a common noun.[9] The problem of the name remains unsolved, or at least not certainly solved. The English name *Hamlet* is another matter. It is often quite incorrectly said to be identical with the name of Saxo's hero, but *Hamlet*, with its variant *Hamnet*, was already a familiar name in Shakespeare's England. Though the Danish name obviously inspired the choice of the similar English name when the old story was reworked for the stage, the names *Hamlet* and *Amleth* are not etymologically related.[10]

Nearly all that we know about the Icelandic Hamlet is related in sources that are much later than Saxo's time. From the Icelander Torfæus (born 1636), who compiled a Danish history, we learn that the story of Amloði was an oral tale and, indeed, that it could still be heard in Iceland in the seventeenth century.

> As regards Saxo's Amleth, when I was a boy in my homeland I heard the story of Amloði told by wretched old men and women and persons of that sort, and at that tender age I regarded it as no more than a tale. But later on when I read Saxo's fuller account, I abandoned my earlier opinion, and from that time on I kept pressuring certain of my friends to look everywhere for the old story, but they wrote me saying that they had no success. At last, a few years ago, I obtained it. I found, however, that it was not at all worth reading, for it was a worthless old wives' tale, and recently composed. It made Amloði not a Dane but a Spaniard! The saga must have been composed after the time of Tamerlane or Tamercutl, for some of the matter is derived from his history.[11]

Hoping to uncover an Icelandic counterpart to Saxo's *Vita Amlethi*, the Icelander was sorely disappointed to find instead a romantic saga. It is regrettable that Torfæus did not choose to record what he recalled of the tale told him in his youth, but happily the romance that disappointed him has survived. It is the *Ambales Saga*, a lying saga (that is, *lygisaga*) composed in the late sixteenth or the seventeenth century.[12] The lying sagas were a popular form of literature that combined features of the native stories of the old heroes with elements of foreign romance. Behind the romantic elaboration in the *Ambales Saga* one can perceive a story that does not differ greatly in its main lines from Saxo's.

> King Salman of Cimbria wed Amba, the daughter of the duke of Burgundy. She bore a son Sigurð. Time passed, and the queen bore another son, who was, however, so big and unsightly that the king refused even to give him a name. Amba called him Ambales. Sigurð grew to be good-looking and skillful, whereas Ambales was ugly and large and would not learn anything worthwhile. The king and his retainers called him Amloði. When the boys were ten and eight years old, Faustinus, a heathen Scythian, and his host attacked Salman and his Christian Cimbrians. The heathens slew most of the

Christians and took captive King Salman and his loyal counselor Gamaliel. Faustinus sent for the king's sons in order that they might see how their father met his death. When Sigurð saw his father on the gallows, he wept, but Ambales laughed gleefully. The heathens were amazed. Then Faustinus asked the elder son how painful it was to look upon that sight, and Sigurð said he hoped to avenge the death. Faustinus had him hanged beside his father. Ambales laughed and pelted his brother as he died. Faustinus said the fool might as well live and be sport for himself and his chieftains.

Faustinus went to Salman's hall, had Gamaliel brought, and asked what would reconcile him to life. Gamaliel's terms were that he be allowed to keep his faith, wealth, rank, and dominion, and that the people be allowed to keep their faith; in turn, they would pay Faustinus tribute and obey him. They exchanged oaths to this effect. Faustinus made himself king of the land, appointed Gamaliel a counselor, and tried unsuccessfully to make Amba his queen. On Gamaliel's advice he held her in honor and let her have her own dwelling. Later he acquired a wife Leta.

Ambales was unlike other men in his ugliness and his behavior. He stayed mostly in the kitchen house and glutted himself. He spoke spitefully to anyone who spoke kindly to him and was kind to anyone who showed him hatred. He did no other work than to whittle long wooden stakes and harden their points in the fire. No one knew what they were for. He seemed like most fools. The king's counselor of old, Addomolus, said that Ambales was full of guile and should be killed before he killed them all. But when the king asked Ambales where he felt the most pain when he saw his father die, the boy answered, "In my buttocks." The heathens laughed, but the Christians grieved.

Wanting Ambales to do something profitable, Faustinus decided that he should stay with the herdsmen and guard the herds. When the herdsmen went to fetch him, he was whittling at his stakes. They asked him what the stakes were for, and Ambales answered, "For avenging my father and not for avenging my father." In the course of the day Ambales made a couple of apparently mad remarks: "The wind has come into the water, and the wind will come out of it again," and "Tonight all the waterfalls will run up, and none down." The king's attempt to make Ambales into a herdsmen proved to be a catastrophic failure. That night there was a terrible storm that drove back all the waterfalls.[13]

Wounded in a fight, Ambales went to his mother's room. The next day, after the men had gone to their work and he and his mother were alone, he told her to bear herself well, though he should put her to great trials. He now spent his evenings in her room. Meanwhile, the king put him in charge of the swine. Addomolus, pointing out that Amloði spent his nights in Amba's room, told Faustinus that Ambales, Amba, and Gamaliel were no doubt conspiring to kill the king. Addomolus said he would soon discover their plans. One evening he went to Amba's room and hid beneath the bed. She and her maids were asleep. When Ambales noticed that Addomolus was not present at the meal in the hall, he rushed to his mother's room. There he ran about, thrusting his spear everywhere. When he heard something beneath the bed, he leapt up on it and thrust his spear down through it. He drowned out the cry with his own voice. While all were asleep, Ambales carried the corpse to the kitchen house, cut it into pieces, put them into the swill and fed it to the swine. The next day the king could not find his counselor. Ambales said:

> I saw a man stuck under a cart,
>   I remember it not;
> Swine did he feed with dainty morsels,
>   I saw the trick.[14]

The men agreed that another must have murdered Addomolus, and Ambales had given his corpse to the swine.

Once Ambales befriended a dwarf, Tosti, who gave him a cloak that made its wearer the handsomest of men. At Ambales' request Tosti secretly cut a hole in each man's seat in the king's hall.

Faustinus, dreaming that Ambales would bring about his death, decided to send Ambales to his brother King Tamerlaus of Scythia. The jarls Cimbal and Carvel escorted him and carried a letter which informed Tamerlaus that the two messengers had been sent to serve Tamerlaus, and with them was a fool, who, if he should behave humanly, should be slain, but otherwise should be allowed to live for the king's amusement. On the journey, while the messengers slept, Ambales replaced the letter with another which bade Tamerlaus take the noble Prince Ambales as his foster son, and explained that the men who accompanied him were his servants. Having donned the magic cloak, Ambales looked very noble. The two jarls were obliged to adopt Christianity and swear fealty to Ambales.

At the banquet Ambales would not eat or drink with the king, although he drank with other men. The king sent a spy to overhear his guests' conversation. Questioned by his two servants, Ambales explained that the grain fields from which the bread had come covered the bones of dead men, so that it was poisonous; the food had been consecrated to idols and was not proper for a Christian to eat; and he did not drink with the king, since the king was the son of a whore. The king, learning of this, found that the field was in fact an old battlefield, and forced his mother Cemeria to acknowledge that his father was actually Duke Artax of India, who begot Tamerlaus on her when her husband King Soldan had gone to war. Ambales wed Tamerlaus's daughter Mesia, who resembled her mother, a Christian.

Now eighteen years old, Ambales sailed back to Cimbria, where he kept his ship at sea until Yule. Tamerlaus's half-brothers Faustinus and Malpriant and their men were celebrating the Yule feast there together. On the eighth day of Yule,[15] when he knew that the drinking would reach its highpoint, Ambales went ashore alone. He put on his old clothes, donned a grotesque fool's mask, placed his stakes in a sack, and went to the hall, where loud reveling could be heard. Everyone was delighted that a fool had come. After playing the fool for a time, he rested beneath the benches, where he stealthily drew down the feasters' cloaks through the holes in the benches and pinned them to the other side with his stakes. The men were drunk and merry. Ambales secretly warned the Christians to leave the hall, and all but Gamaliel did so. Suddenly Ambales picked up Gamaliel and carried him outside. The hall was set on fire, and all two thousand men inside were burnt to death. Then Ambales released Gamaliel.

The next day Ambales called a public meeting, in which he declared his right to the land, and the chieftains acknowledged it, so that he was made king. He fetched his wife home. Later he became king of France and ruled until he died.

In both the *Ambales Saga* and the *Vita Amlethi* (*a*) the hero's father, king of the land, is slain by another man who (*b*) assumes the throne and (*c*) weds, or attempts to wed, the widowed queen. The hero (*d*) prudently plays the fool in self-defense and (*e*) passes his time whittling crooks or stakes at the hearth. He accumulates a store of them and guards them carefully. No one knows their purpose, though in fact (*f*) the hero reveals it in obscure language; for he prefers generally to acknowledge the truth in all things, though his position of relative weakness requires that he do so in a metaphoric or other riddling manner. The king and his men harbor uneasy doubts about the reality of the boy's apparent witlessness. Their anxiety is expressed in a series of three episodes which, explicitly or not, test the hero. The first incident is quite dissimilar in the two accounts, perhaps because Ambales, as a Christian, must not be permitted to indulge in nonmarital sexual relations, though it does happen in both that (*g*) the king's men take the hero with them into the woods or the wild, for they wish to observe whether he responds normally to a woman (Saxo), or they try him out as a herdsman (saga). It is in this episode that (*h*) the hero speaks cryptically about storms: Amleth refers to the stormy sea as a mill that long ago ground the sand, and Ambales obscurely foretells a coming storm. The second test (*i*) is set in the queen's room, where the king's spy hides himself in order to overhear what the hero and his mother say. But (*j*) the youth kills him and feeds his corpse to the swine. When asked about the man, (*k*) the hero explains the matter in riddling words that everyone fails to understand.

In the meantime, however, *(l)* he reveals his mind to his mother. In the final test (*m*) the hero is sent out of the country, for the king considers him to be too dangerous to keep at home. On the journey (*n*) he secretly rewrites the letter carried by his two escorts, so that upon their arrival the foreign monarch receives the hero well. The youth (*o*) astonishes everyone by his marvelous sensitivity and perception at the royal banquet, and eventually (*p*) marries the king's daughter. His two escorts (*q*) are executed or become his servants. After a time (*r*) he returns home, where the king and his men are celebrating the hero's funeral (Saxo) or the heathen festival of Yule (saga). The youth (*s*) enters the hall and plays the fool while the men drink heavily. The hero (*t*) binds them all together with his crooks or nails their clothes to their benches with his stakes, and sets fire to the hall. After (*u*) the people acknowledge his claim to the throne he (*v*) fetches his wife home and reigns until his death. The saga has nothing that answers to the later adventures of Amleth.

These stories are made up of an introductory portion, which details the problems brought about by the villain together with the hero's immediate response, and a conclusion, which answers to the initial problems by giving the hero's eventual solution. The solution is delayed by a middle section that explores the tension between the villain and the hero. The main elements of the Hamlet story can be described in outline as follows:

FRONT FRAME

1. Murder
2. Throne
3. Marriage
4. Hero as fool

CENTRAL TENSION

5. Woods episode
6. Bedroom episode
7. Foreign-land episode

BACK FRAME

8. Revenge
9. Throne

Although it cannot be known with certainty whether the composer of the saga was influenced, directly or indirectly, by Saxo's account of Amleth, I find no reason to suppose that the work is anything other than a literary treatment of a native story by an Icelander. Indeed, on occasion the details of an incident common to both compositions are less coherent in the Danish history than in the Icelandic saga, so the later work can actually serve to illuminate obscurities in the earlier (Commentary, sec.5), a fact which suggests that the saga is independent of Saxo. No one doubts that there still existed a living Hamlet tradition in Iceland, for the testimony of Torfæus, who remembered hearing as a child the tale of Amloði, is proof that there was. Whatever the tale was, it was similar enough to Saxo's *Vita Amlethi* that Torfæus, after he had grown up and read Saxo, connected the two heroes in his mind. Nor can anyone doubt that the composer of the saga did in fact draw upon local tradition for his saga, at least in part. This much is proved by the amusing little tale of Brjam, which was collected in Iceland from an old woman, Hildur Arngrímsdóttir, in 1707.[16]

The tale relates how the king of a land killed a poor old man for the sake of his excellent cow, which the king coveted.

> The old man had seven sons, of whom Brjam was the eldest. When the king's men killed their father, the children all wept except for Brjam, and when they were asked where they felt the most pain, the others struck their chests but Brjam slapped his buttocks and grinned. The men killed Brjam's brothers but spared him, since they thought him a fool. After a number of adventures Brjam went to a smithy, carved some wooden stakes, and proceeded to a banquet that the king was enjoying with his friends. The boy quietly nailed each person's clothes to the floor. When the guests could not rise, they blamed one

> another, began to fight, and killed one another. The next day Brjam went to the palace and offered himself to the queen as a servant. She gladly hired him, for she had few left. He did well, married the princess, and became king.

Hildur's tale shows that certain features of the *Ambales Saga*, such as the hero's apparently idiotic response to his father's death and his employment of stakes rather than crooks for his revenge, reflect the Icelandic story tradition in general rather than the invention of this composer in particular. There is no need to assume that the writer drew upon Saxo's *Vita Amlethi.*

However fascinating they are in their own right, the Icelandic Hamlet texts are all too early or too late to illustrate what the Icelandic tradition was like when Saxo was composing his narrative. Times and tastes and tellers changed, and details of the story evidently changed with them. The old incident about the sand as Amloði's meal (Commentary, sec.4) is absent from the saga, as also are all the other Icelandic borrowings that scholars have seen, or thought they have seen, in Saxo's composition (Commentary, sec.3, 10). What the saga does show, if its independence from Saxo is granted, is that Saxo has not radically restructured the story for his own purposes, for in the presence and sequence of major episodes the *Vita Amlethi* and the *Ambales Saga* are in essential agreement.

There is no evidence for the Hamlet story as an oral narrative outside of Denmark and Iceland. It may have been told elsewhere, of course, and probably was, but of that we know nothing. What we can say with some certainty is only that the story was familiar in one place or another in the North for over six centuries, from around 1000 when the skald Snæbjörn alludes to "Amloði's meal," to Torfæus's reminiscence of hearing the tale during his childhood in the first half of the seventeenth century. How old the tale already was in Snæbjörn's time or just what the tale was like then, it is impossible to say. Neither do we know what developments the story underwent after Torfæus's day, before people ceased telling it altogether. For it is a fact that it no longer belongs to the repertoire of oral storytellers. If we count the tale of Brjam as a part of the Hamlet tradition, as hero legend transformed into folktale, then the old story could actually still be heard as recently as the nineteenth century.[17] That is all we are able to say in outline about the history of the Hamlet story in oral tradition, relying as we must upon the written retellings of it and the allusions to it that we chance to have.

Two: The Hero as Fool

Does the Hamlet story stand entirely alone in oral tradition as a creation without family ties, or is it simply one form of a more widely spread story? If the latter is true, the history of the stories to which it is genetically related is also part of its own history, and drawing upon them we should be able to go beyond the impasse that we reached in our inquiry into the Hamlet tradition in Scandinavia. Unfortunately, the question of Hamlet's affinity with other traditional heroes remains to be settled, for despite many scholarly contributions to the problem, there is little consensus on the answer. Some of the suggested analogues to Hamlet, such as Telemachos, are farfetched and unconvincing, and most of the others (for example, Orestes, Havelok the Dane), though they seem possible, lack sufficient points of similarity with Hamlet to permit us to be certain one way or the other.[1] Indeed, probably no likely analogue has been proposed by one scholar which has not also been dismissed by another scholar.

I shall attempt to cast some light on this matter by comparing the Hamlet story with what I regard as its two closest and only certain relatives. What I hope to show in principle is that the story did not come into being and pass away without kin (though in any case no student of oral story will fail to perceive general similarities between it and many other hero legends),[2] but rather is a particular development of an international story known also outside the

North. The principal fault of the comparisons that have been made in the past is that they have dwelt upon a small number of surface resemblances, and the same can be said of the critiques that have been leveled against them. It seems worthwhile therefore to treat the question in some detail here.

The Legend of H and H

The Scandinavian story that is most reminiscent of the Hamlet tradition is a legend that was roughly contemporary with that tradition. The fullest accounts are found in Saxo's *Gesta Danorum* and in a *fornaldarsaga*, the *Saga of Hrolf Kraki*.[3]

> According to Saxo (7.1.1–7), when King Olaf of Denmark lay dying, he bade his sons Frodi and Harald rule, the one over the land and the other over the sea, in yearly alternation. First Frodi was the sea king, but he suffered continual defeats. When, however, Harald ruled the sea, he was very successful, and so earned his brother's hatred. In addition, their queens Signe and Ulfhild quarreled constantly about which was the nobler, so that they broke up their husbands' households. Frodi and Harald divided up the goods they held in common. But Frodi, judging that his brother's glory was his disgrace, had one of his men secretly kill Harald. To appear innocent, he ordered an investigation into Harald's sudden death, but the common people continued silently to condemn Frodi. Frodi then sought to kill Harald and Halfdan, the sons of Harald and Signe, but their foster parents cunningly saved them. While making it appear that the boys had been devoured by wolves, they actually put the boys in a hollow oak tree, gave them dogs' names, and for a long time fed them under the pretense that they were dogs.
>
> Frodi alone refused to believe they were dead. From a woman skilled in divination he learned that Regin was secretly rearing them and concealing the fact by giving them the names of dogs. After Regin found that the speculation concerning him and his wards was becoming the subject of common talk,

he took them to Fyn. But Frodi captured him there. He begged the king to spare the boys, since it was he who had rendered them fatherless. Regin promised that if they should conceive any plot, he would inform the king. He won their safety thereby and lived many years without fear. When the two boys grew up and went to Zealand, their friends urged them to avenge their father. They made the vow that they and their uncle would not both live out the year. When Regin learned this, he went at night to the royal estate to fulfill his agreement with the king. There he said that he had come secretly to tell the king something he had promised. But Frodi was asleep, and it was not permitted to disturb the king's slumber.

In the morning Frodi heard of the visit from his sentries, and, understanding that Regin had come to tell him of a plot, he gathered his men together. Harald and Halfdan had no choice then but to feign madness. Attacked by Frodi's men, they behaved like maniacs, and Frodi, believing they were demented, called off the attack. He thought it shameful to attack with the sword persons who were turning their swords against themselves. But the following night Harald and Halfdan attacked the royal hall, first crushing the queen under a pile of stones and then setting fire to the building.[4] Frodi was forced to crawl into some dark and narrow tunnels, where the smoke suffocated him. After Frodi's death Halfdan reigned as king of Denmark.

The story continues, but we shall not pursue it beyond this point. The *Saga of Hrolf Kraki*, in a different version of what obviously is essentially the same tale, gives the heroes the names Hroar and Helgi. The saga was composed about two centuries after Saxo wrote. Here also I consider only the first half of the story.

According to the saga (chaps. 1–4), there were two brothers, Halfdan and Froði, each of whom ruled his own kingdom. King Halfdan was good-natured, but king Froði was savage. Halfdan had one daughter Signy, wed to Jarl Sævil, and two young sons, Hroar and Helgi. The boys' foster father was named Regin. King Halfdan ruled Denmark alone but was the object of much envy from King Froði, who considered his own lot to be less fortunate. And so he gathered an army and went to Denmark, where he slew King Halfdan and forced the folk to swear allegiance to himself. Regin escaped with Helgi and Hroar, taking them to a nearby island where he asked Vifil, an old friend of King Halfdan, to guard the boys from King Froði. The boys stayed in an underground room at night, but spent the days in the woods. Since Regin had family and land in Denmark, he himself had little choice but to go to Froði and swear allegiance to him.

Froði was ill at ease, however, because he had not found Hroar and Helgi. Though he promised rewards to their finders and torture to their keepers, he found out nothing. The magicians told him that the boys were not far away, yet not on that land. The king searched Vifil's island but without success, for Vifil had previously arranged it with the boys that if he called to his dogs Hop and Ho, they should hide in their earth house. But after the third search Vifil told the boys that he would send them to their kinsman Sævil.

Hroar and Helgi left. Using the names Ham and Hrani, they came to Jarl Sævil's hall, and he agreed to let them stay awhile. No one knew who they were. Many thought they had scurvy, since they always kept their heads partially hooded. Thus they stayed for three years.

It then happened that King Froði invited the jarl to a feast, for Froði suspected that he might be hiding his young kinsmen Hroar and Helgi. The jarl's wife, Signy, and many men accompanied him, but he did not give the boys permission to come along. But Ham (that is, Helgi) seized an unbroken colt and rode after them, turning his face to the horse's tail and acting like a fool. Hrani (Hroar) got a manageable horse and rode it the proper way. But the boys were unable to control their steeds, with the result that Hrani's hood was shaken off. His sister recognized him and informed the jarl. He replied that that was good news but their identity must not become known. When they reached the banquet the boys ran back and forth in the hall. Their sister, Signy, quietly warned them not to remain there, since they were not yet men, but they paid no attention to her. A witch named Heið came. During a feast in her honor she revealed that they who once on Vifil's island were called by the names of dogs were present in the hall. Signy tried to bribe the sorceress, but Froði forced her to continue. Heið said that Hroar and Helgi would kill Froði unless they themselves were quickly slain, and that Ham and Hrani were they. But she warned the boys before she herself ran away, and the boys fled from the hall in fear. Their foster father Regin recognized them. The king bade his men look for them, but Regin extinguished the lights, and some of the king's men who wanted the boys to escape held the others back so that the boys were able to reach the woods. Froði said that they should drink the night long, for Hroar and Helgi, happy to have gotten away, would make good their escape. Regin and many of his friends eagerly plied the ale so that the men fell down on one another in a drunken sleep.

Regin rode out into the woods after them. When the brothers recognized their foster father, they happily greeted him. He did not return the greeting, but rode back toward the hall. The boys puzzled over the meaning of this. Then he turned his horse around again and rode to them, acting as though he were angry and wanted to fight with them. Regin now rode back towards the hall again, and they followed. Helgi understood that their foster father acted thus because he did not wish to break his oath to King Froði, and so would not talk with them, but he wanted to help them. When they reached some trees near the king's hall, Regin said, as if to himself, "If I had a great grievance against King Froði, I would set fire to these trees." Helgi understood that he wanted them to set fire to the hall and prevent all but their friends from coming out. Helgi decided that they must chance their luck if they wanted revenge.

Then Jarl Sævil and his men came out of the hall. He said that he had no obligation to King Froði and suggested to his men that they help the boys by heaping up the fire. Regin also came out with his men. Within the hall King Froði now awoke. At that moment they heard Regin outside the door of the hall speaking a verse:

> Regin is outside
> And so are the warriors of Halfdan,
> Brave fighters:
> Let Froði be told.
> Var forged nails,
> And Var put heads on them,
> And Var drove for Var
> A nail of precaution.

Inside, the king's men said that it was no great news if there was rain outside or if the king's smiths (the king had two smiths, both called Var) plied their craft, whether they were now making nails or anything else. But the king understood that Regin was warning him.[5] He went to the door and saw that there was trouble outside. The whole hall then began to blaze. Froði went from the door to the entrance of his earth house,[6] thinking that he would escape to the woods, but when he reached the earth house, Regin was waiting in a hostile mood. The king turned back and with many of his men was burnt to death within the hall. Also Sigrið, mother of Hroar and Helgi, was burnt to death, since she would not go out.[7] The two brothers took over the kingdom. Helgi became king.

Several important elements that appear in both narratives—the witch who reveals the whereabouts and the disguises of the boys, the foster father's oath, the heroes' playing the fool—do not occupy comparable slots in the sequence of events, so that although the two versions of the story share essentially the same plot, some features have obviously shifted form, function, or place in the course of time and tellings.[8] On the whole the Icelandic text is much the fuller, both in the details of the narration and in the number of the episodes. It has also partially assimilated an international folktale (Type 502),[9] which has enriched (or perhaps confused) the middle of the narrative with some new elements. Saxo's account shows no trace of it. But I am more interested here in whether the features that are common both to the story of H and H and to the story of Hamlet are such that a historical connection of some sort seems likely. In the summary comparison that follows, the presence of a trait in the Hamlet tradition is indicated by *A* (= Amleth) or *a* (= Ambales), in the other tradition by *H* (= Harald and Halfdan) or *h* (= Hroar and Helgi). For grammatical simplicity the term "hero" includes both hero and heroes.

In most of the the texts (*AHh*), the story is localized in Denmark; in one (*a*), it is centered in or near Denmark. In the front frame (1) a king is murdered (*AaHh*) by his jealous brother (*AHh*). The slayer (2) assumes the throne (*AaHh*) and (3) weds, or tries to wed, the widowed queen (*AaH?h*). (4) The son or sons of the murdered king regularly (*Aa*) or occasionally (*Hh*) play the fool. Two texts explain the origin of the murderer's jealousy in the same, rather unusual way (*AH*): at their father's death the two brothers both succeed him, the one becoming the sea king, the other the land king; but the signal success of the sea king causes the other to envy him his glory. (For a fuller discussion see the Commentary, sec. 1.)

After his father's murder there is an understandable concern for the hero's safety, but here the two traditions employ different devices for his defense. Amleth/Ambales remains in the hall with his enemies, his defense being his constant disguise as a fool by which he pretends that he is no threat to anyone. H and H are instead rescued from the hall by their foster father and live elsewhere in disguise. The device that safeguards the hero determines in turn the particular nature of the villain's activity. The one villain tests; the other seeks. Though all the texts contain the theme of feigned foolishness, it is more important in the Hamlet tradition in which it is the hero's sole defense.

The Hamlet story develops the tension between the protagonist and antagonist in three successive episodes that I have labeled the woods, bedroom, and foreign-land episodes. It has not been noticed that the central episode of the H and H story is parallel in important ways to the woods incident in the Amleth legend; but the relationship is complex.

(5) Suspecting that his nephew is playing the fool (*A*) or that his nephews are hiding in the house of a kinsman (*h*), the king arranges to test the nephew or the kinsman in order to learn the truth (*Ah*). (6) When the hero sets out with the other men, he rides his steed backwards (*Ah*) and generally behaves in a foolish (*A*) or childish (*h*) way. (7) The king confronts him with a woman who penetrates or is about to penetrate his disguise (*Ah*), but (8) he is warned of the danger (*Ah*) so that he and the woman flee into the woods (*Ah*). Back at the hall (9) the foster brother or foster father speaks in a riddling manner to the king's men, who fail to catch his point (*Ah*; compare also *H*); only the hero (*A*) or the king (*Hh*) understands the true message.

While these features are parallel both in theme and in relative sequence, several other important elements are thematically similar but show dissimilar positions within their episodes. Since it is impossible to integrate them into the list without obscuring the sequence of action that is common to both traditions, I mention them separately. These elements concern the hero's foster sister or sister and his foster brother or foster father, who are prominent in this episode. These characters individually recognize the hero's true identity behind his disguise of fool or stranger and make a gesture of support. Thus, (10) the foster sister learns from the hero's normal behavior that he is merely playing the fool (*A*), or the sister recognizes the hero when his hood is shaken off (*h*), and (11) she conspires with him (*A*) or with her husband (*h*) to keep the hero's secret. The male figure makes a more peculiar contribution. (12) The foster brother knows that the hero is playing the fool (*A*), or the foster father recognizes the hero's identity (*h*); (13) following him to the woods, the foster brother / foster father sends him a secret, metaphoric message (*Ah*), which (14) the hero correctly decodes (*Ah*).

Whereas the Hamlet story now continues with two additional episodes before allowing the hero his revenge, the simpler tale of H and H proceeds directly to the revenge episode. In the back frame,

(15) the hero plays the idiot for his enemies, turning his sword against himself (*AH*). (16) The king and his men are gathered in the hall drinking deeply (*AaH?h*). (17) After the hero's allies slip out of the hall (*ah*), the hero sets fire to it, killing all the men within (*AaHh*), but (18) the king himself perishes nearby in his tent (*A*) or tunnel (*H*; compare *h*). (19) The hero assumes the throne (*AaHh*).

The two stories thus agree in the general course of the plot—the fratricide, the villain's taking his brother's throne and wife, the hero's pretended idiocy, his eventual firing of the hall and accession to the throne—and in one central adventure, the woods episode, which tells of the villain's employment of a woman to penetrate the hero's identity and of the help the latter receives from a kinswoman and a kinsman. In addition, the tales are linked by the presence of several rather unusual features, such as the horse that is ridden backwards, which appears at the beginning of the corresponding episode in each story. In view of this analysis, it would require considerable faith to believe that these stories developed independently of each other. Accordingly, the old assertion of Olrik and his followers that the two stories are unrelated, the motifs of the wrongly ridden horse and of the pretended madness in the H and H tradition being merely isolated and incompetent borrowings from the Hamlet legend, is untenable.[10] Olrik's view is founded upon a superficial analysis of the stories and does not take into account the numerous other parallels in structure and motif. It is also based upon the unproved assumption, which was especially popular in the nineteenth century, that narrative inconsistencies and awkwardnesses are evidence of borrowing and interpolation.[11]

Since it is necessary to posit a connection of some kind in order to explain the extensive correspondences between the narratives, the question now becomes what kind of relationship it is that obtains between them. The first investigator to deal at some length with the two stories, Ferdinand Detter, concludes that the two traditions are historically related, and simply assumes, without considering other possibilities, that the H and H tradition is a development of the Hamlet story.[12] He offers no argument or evidence for his assumption, nor, in truth, does he place much emphasis on the derivation. But Elton, who follows him in his conclusion that the stories are closely related, points out that either could be the parent story, or it could be the case that neither is, that they are, rather, collateral variants that ultimately derive from some earlier form of the story, an explanation that in fact he deems more likely.[13] This is as fair a statement of the case as I can imagine. There are three logical possibilities, none of which appears to be capable of proof, though the third, because it is more general than the others, seems likeliest.

The Legend of Brutus

Outside of the North the traditional hero most similar to Hamlet is found in Roman tradition. The Romans numbered among their ancient heroes Lucius Junius Brutus, who drove out the last king of Rome and founded the republic, traditionally in 509 B.C. No doubt the legend of the original Brutus was attached to the gens Iunia partly to provide an etiology for its strange cognomen, which, whatever it may once have signified, was popularly interpreted as being identical with the ordinary adjective *brutus* 'dull, stupid'. This story not only claimed that the Junian family earned the nickname from its cleverness rather than from its stupidity, but it also declared that the family played a glorious role in the early history of Rome.

The fullest versions of the Brutus legend that we have are the well-known Latin narrative of Livy (*Histories* I.39–60) from the late first century B.C. and the Greek account of Dionysios of Halikarnassos (*Roman Antiquities,* bk. 4) from the end of the same century. Since the two historians mostly agree on the course of the events, I give here a single, synthetic summary of the legend. As before, I limit myself to the first half of the hero's biography.

> King Tarquinius Priscus and his wife Tanaquil reigned at Rome. They had two sons, Arruns and Lucius, and two daughters.

They also raised a fatherless boy, Servius Tullius, as though he were their own son, and eventually gave him their daughter Tarquinia in marriage. On the death of King Tarquinius, Servius acted as king. Servius anticipated that Arruns and Lucius might resent him; with this in mind he gave them his two daughters in marriage. Later Servius asked the people to confirm his right to the throne. Unfortunately, the ambitious Lucius was wed to the unambitious daughter of Servius, whereas his mild-mannered brother Arruns was wed to her ambitious sister. But Lucius and his sister-in-law Tullia conspired, brought about the deaths of their spouses, and wed each other. She then prodded Lucius on against her own father Servius. After he had increased his influence, Lucius Tarquinius and an armed guard went to the Forum, where he sat on the king's throne and called himself king. He and his men killed King Servius. Thus began the reign of L. Tarquinius, whose tyrannical behavior earned him the cognomen Superbus, that is, the Overbearing or the Proud.

Having no legal title to the throne, Tarquinius ruled by fear and force. He tried capital cases by his own authority, punishing with death, exile, or confiscation of property men whom he suspected or disliked or whose property he desired. Among the men he murdered was Marcus Junius, husband of the king's sister Tarquinia. Marcus was secretly slain, not for any crime, but for his wealth. He also killed Marcus's elder son, who showed signs of a noble spirit and of a will to avenge his father's murder.[14] Marcus's younger son Lucius, seeing the fates of his father and his brother and many other Roman nobles, and being then only a youth, decided to show no sign of intelligence for the king to fear and to possess no wealth for him to covet. He feigned stupidity, acquiring the nickname Brutus. Tarquinius took from him his inheritance. The contempt in which he was held was his protection. Furthermore, King Tarquinius kept Brutus under his own authority on the grounds that he was an orphan who still required guardians. He had Brutus live with his own children, not (as he alleged) to do him honor as a kinsman, but in order that Brutus might amuse his children by his foolish speech and acts.

In the course of time there was a frightful portent (Livy) or a plague (Dionysios).[15] Tarquinius decided to dispatch his sons Titus and Arruns to make inquiry at Apollo's oracle at Delphi and sent with them Brutus as a butt for their amusement. Brutus carried with him, as an offering for Apollo, a gold-filled stick, which was a figurative symbol of his mind (Livy); Tarquinius's sons laughed at Brutus for offering only a wooden stick, since it had no value so far as anyone could see (Dionysios).[16] After they had transacted the business for which they had been sent, Titus and Arruns asked the oracle which of them would be the next king of Rome. The oracle replied: "He who shall be the first to kiss his mother shall hold supreme authority in Rome." The two brothers drew lots to determine which of them, upon their return, should kiss their mother first (Livy), or they agreed to kiss her simultaneously (Dionysios); but Brutus alone understood the true sense of the oracle, and, pretending to trip, he kissed the earth, mother of all creatures.[17] They returned to Rome.

Soon thereafter the Romans began siege operations at the town of Ardea. One day the young princes were drinking in the quarters of Sextus Tarquinius, another of King Tarquinius's sons.[18] Among them there was Tarquinius Collatinus, son of Egerius. The subject of their wives arose, and each man praised his own. Collatinus suggested that they might prove the superiority of his own wife Lucretia in a few hours by riding off to their homes, for there was no better proof than what a man finds when he returns unannounced. They all agreed and galloped off to Rome, arriving at dusk, and found the wives of the princes enjoying themselves at a luxurious party; proceeding to the town of Collatia, however, they found Lucretia busy at her wool work. She clearly won the competition. But her beauty and purity aroused Sextus Tarquinius, who determined to debauch her by force. The men returned to camp. A few days later Sextus returned to Lucretia's house, where he was hospitably received. That night, while the household was asleep, he made his way to Lucretia's room and forced her to have sexual relations with him. Then he left.

Lucretia sent to her father and her husband, bidding them come quickly with a trusted friend. Her father came with P. Valerius, her husband with Brutus, with whom he had chanced to be when the messenger found him. The woman recounted what had happened, urged them to avenge her, refused to excuse herself, stabbed herself, and fell dead. Brutus drew the knife out and cried: "By this chaste blood and by the gods, I swear that I will punish L. Tarquinius Superbus, his wicked wife, and all his children, and never again shall I permit them or any other to be king in Rome." The others looked at him in astonishment at this sign of intelligence. They swore similarly and followed him as their leader.

Lucretia's body was brought to the forum, where an angry crowd gathered. Brutus urged them to take up arms. Led by him, the populace marched on Rome. As tribune of the knights, Brutus had the people summoned and reminded them of the various crimes that the royal family had committed. The people demanded an end to the king's authority and the exile of the royal family. Brutus then went to Ardea, where he incited the army against the king. The Tarquinii were driven into exile; Sextus was slain. The reign of Tarquinius Superbus had ended and with it the monarchy at Rome. In place of a king, two consuls were elected by popular vote. The first consuls were Brutus and Collatinus.

Let us compare this Roman legend with the Hamlet story to determine the extent and the nature of the correspondence between them. The initial events in the Roman tale are more complicated than in the Northern story. Tarquinius commits many murders rather than one, none of them corresponding exactly to the crime of Amleth's uncle Fengi, whose victim is at once the husband of the woman he takes, the reigning monarch, and the father of the hero. These three elements are in fact present also in the Roman story, but they occur, rather, in succession. L. Tarquinius commits three major murders. First, he kills his own brother and weds his widowed sister-in-law. This fratricide and marriage correspond to Fengi's fratricide and marriage with Geruth. Next, Lucius kills his quasi-foster brother King Servius and usurps his throne. The regicide corresponds to Fengi's regicide and rule. And third, he murders his brother-in-law Marcus Junius, father of Brutus, which murder is parallel to Fengi's murder of Amleth's father. Of Tarquinius's three murders, then, the first gives him access to the woman he wants, the second gives him access to the throne, and the third gives him wealth and, on a different level, motivates the hero to act. It is as if the one victim in the Danish story were analyzed here into his aspects of husband, king, and father. All three murders are forms of fratricide, the result of them being that Tarquinius entirely disposes of the fraternal element in his family. In the following summary comparisons, the presence of a feature in the Hamlet tradition is indicated, as before, by *A* (= Amleth) or *a* (= Ambales), and in the Brutus tradition by *B*.

In the front frame (1) the jealous villain murders his brother the king (*A*) or his brother and the king and his brother-in-law (*B*). He (2) weds the widow (*AB*) and (3) assumes the throne (*AaB*). Whereas (4) one nephew is spirited and threatens revenge and so is killed along with his father (*aB*), (5) the other prudently plays the fool in self-defense and is spared (*AaB*). (6) He acquires the nickname Amloði or Brutus, that is, Fool (*aB*). (7) The hero dwells in the royal house with his uncle the king (*AB*).

The next episode in the Brutus tale, the trip to Apollo at Delphi, obviously corresponds to Amleth's voyage to the king of Britain and Ambales' journey to the king of Scythia, which I call the foreign-land episode. The more obvious parallels have long been noticed—the hero's foreign journey, his companions, his gold-filled stick(s)—but it has gone unnoticed that there is a whole sequence of structural similarities beneath the surface.

(8) Anxious for his safety, the king dispatches two agents on a mission to a foreign land (*AaB*). (9) They bear a secret message from the king to a foreign lord, namely, a letter for the king (*Aa*) or a query for the god (*B*). (10) The message is prompted by the

king's anxiety for his life and throne (*AaB*). (11) The agents also escort the hero, whom the king sent along to be victim (*Aa*) or fool (*aB*). But (12) the hero devises a secret message of his own: he rewrites their runic stick (*A*) or letter (*a*) or carries a symbolic stick (*B*). (13)This message informs the foreign lord of the hero's excellence (*AaB*). (14) They reach the foreign land and deliver their messages (*AaB*). (15) The lord responds, the king with a banquet (*Aa*), the god with an oracle (*B*), as though to test the hero's proclaimed self-evaluation. (16) The hero alone perceives the subtle impurities in the banquet (*Aa*) or the metaphoric sense of the oracle (*B*), whereas (17) the two agents mistakenly find the banquet to be faultless (*Aa*) or interpret the oracle literally (*B*), and so mock the hero as a fool when he relates what he perceived (*A*) or when he acts upon his interpretation (*B*).[19] In the end (18) the expected fates of the hero and the king's agents are exactly reversed, for the hero (= intended victim) wins his life (*Aa*) while they lose theirs (*A*), or he wins a divine guarantee of rule while they (= intended successors) lose their chance of rule (*B*). With or without his companions (19) the hero returns home (*AaB*).

The remaining central episode is the famous story of Lucretia, in which one can perceive an old Roman legend type that one might call *The Lustful Patrician*. In this tale (i) a lustful patrician, representing an institution or a law, tries unfairly to obtain a modest and attractive maid or lad; (ii) the youth is killed or beaten; but (iii) the folk are so outraged that (iv) the institution associated with the patrician comes to an end. In addition to Sextus and Lucretia, the story is told of Appius Claudius and Virginia and of Lucius Papirius and Gaius Publilius.[20] Although the Lucretia story is placed earlier in Roman traditional history, there is no reason to assume that it is the original and the others are copies or derivatives of it. On the other hand, there is no reason to suppose that this tale was inserted entire into the Brutus legend; more likely, the plot of the Lustful Patrician merely influenced an already extant episode to which it was similar, so that the Lucretia episode as we have it probably represents the confluence of several stories. No one has perceived that there are resemblances between this episode and the woods and bedroom episodes of the Hamlet story. The woods episode centers on a test, the Northern tradition emphasizing the testing of a man, the Southern the testing of a woman.

(20) It is decided to conduct a test of the hero's sexual response to a woman (*A*) or of a woman's fidelity to her husband (*B*). (21) The testers proceed on horseback to the woods where the woman awaits (*A*) or to her house (*B*). They arrive, and (22) the beautiful woman arouses the sexual passion of the hero (*A*) or of another king's son (*B*). (23) He presently has sexual intercourse with her in secret (*AB*). Subsequently (24) she reveals that he ravished her (*AB*); nevertheless, (25) the hero or the woman passes the original test, for no one credits her confession (*A*) or she follows her confession with suicide (*B*).

At this point, resemblances between the woods incident of the Danish legend and the Lucretia episode of the Roman legend fade out. The Hamlet story continues with the bedroom episode, which also shows parallels to the Lucretia tale, especially the latter half of it, as though the Lucretia tale was created through the fusion of two independent episodes, or the two episodes resulted from the fission of a once-unified tale.

(26) The king (*A*) or his son (*B*) has sexual relations with a woman. (27) After he departs, the hero comes to her room (*Aa*) or house (*B*). (28) She is reproached by the hero for her sexual misconduct (*A*), or she reproaches herself for her sexual misconduct (*B*).[21] (29)The hero drops his disguise, revealing that his folly is only feigned and that he desires revenge (*AB*).

Finally, in the back frame (30) the hero removes the king through death (*Aa*) or exile (*B*), and (31) succeeds him (*AaB*). Like Amleth, Brutus addresses the people, revealing how he played the fool and reviewing the villainy of the king; but Brutus's speech precedes the disposal of the king, and Amleth's follows it.

That the stories of Hamlet and Brutus resemble each other has long been noticed and was doubtless apparent to Saxo himself, but Detter was the first scholar to discuss the resemblances in some detail and to offer a theory to account for the dozen or so parallels he perceived. He argues that the Roman story was the model for the Scandinavian story. The Brutus story reached the North where it was transformed into the Hamlet story by a Scandinavian *Bearbeiter*, who, Detter seems to believe, worked from written sources. What could be retained was retained; what could not (for example, the Delphic oracle) was adapted. Marion Taylor has restated Detter's view of the relationship of the stories, suggesting, however, that the tale was brought to Scandinavia by Varangians. But Elton, as before, is disinclined to accept a simple and direct derivation of the one story from the other. He points out that there is no need to assume that the Hamlet story is a classical story transformed, and observes that the Scandinavian and Roman versions may be "separate offshoots" of a European story. Otto Jiriczek similarly rejects the idea that one of the stories is a direct copy of the other, and thinks the best explanation is that of a wandering oral story that has appeared in different places.[22] So we are back to the familiar opposition: collateral or derivative?

As if that were not difficult enough, there is a third view according to which Saxo himself, when he was setting down his account of Amleth's life, increased its resemblance with the Brutus legend by incorporating motifs from the latter into the former. Now, there is no question whatsoever that Saxo knew the Brutus tale, at least in part, for a summary of a portion of the story, about a paragraph in length, is given by Valerius Maximus (*Memorable Saying and Deeds* 7. 2), whom we know Saxo read. Indeed, Saxo borrowed many a phrase from Valerius, as a glance at the bottom of virtually any page in Olrik's and Ræder's edition of the *Gesta Danorum* will show. That being the case, it is hardly surprising that he adapted some unconnected phrases from Valerius's account of Brutus to his own narrative of Amleth. But that is quite a different thing from importing actual content into his narrative from Valerius, and any attempt to explain the parallels between the two tradions in this fashion leads to absurdity. For example, Gollancz (who accepts the kinship of the stories) says that the presence in both stories of the motif of gold concealed inside of a hollowed-out stick cannot be due to coincidence; rather, Saxo must have borrowed it from Valerius because Saxo borrowed at least one phrase from Valerius's Brutus for his own Amleth.[23] But it does not follow, of course, that an author who borrows collocations of words from his stylistic models also borrows plot elements; nor are borrowing and coincidence the only explanations available to us, since the shared trait can be accounted for equally well by the assumption that the tales are genetically collaterals. Gollancz also ignores the fact that though Amleth and Brutus both employ gold-filled sticks in similar episodes, Amleth does not, like Brutus, carry his as a secret gift or message *for* the foreign lord, which one might expect him to do if Saxo simply transferred a trait from Brutus directly to Amleth; instead, Amleth brings it *back* from the foreign country to his own land, a variation that more readily suggests one of the little shifts of function and place that a motif may undergo in oral storytelling than a deliberate change introduced by a literary compiler. The motif is familiar from oral folktales: a cunnning debtor gives a gold-filled stick to his creditor and then claims that he has repaid his debt.[24] This corresponds more closely to Amleth's trick than it does to Brutus's, which is hard to explain if, following Gollancz, we imagine that Amleth learned the trick from Brutus; for if the motif was borrowed ultimately from an international folktale, which seems likely, and if the Roman story passed it on to the Danish story, as Gollancz believes, then we should hardly expect the motif as it appears in the *Vita Amlethi* to be closer to the motif as it appears in the oral folktale. Brutus gives a gold-filled stick to Apollo as a gift and / or message, whereas Amleth brings two sticks filled with wergild with him back to Denmark as replacements for the king's two agents, whose deaths Amleth has engineered, and actually shows them to the king's men when they ask him where his companions are. That is to say, he acts somewhat as though he is returning the two men to their fellows, as a debtor to his creditors.

The theory of borrowed motifs encounters still other problems. Gollancz, observing that Valerius does not mention the murder of Brutus's father, now assumes that Saxo also read some unknown historian who does mention this feature of the story! One may observe, however, that although Valerius does mention the murder of Brutus's *brother*, Saxo has not adopted from him this excellent motif for his narrative. Again, Gollancz is certain that Saxo has access also to Livy's history, since the distribution of the *Vita Amlethi* over books 3 and 4 of the *Gesta Danorum* seems to Gollancz to be similar to Livy's arrangement of the Brutus narrative in his books 1 and 2.[25] But is it likely that Saxo or any other intelligent author has ever composed in the fashion which the theory of borrowed motifs assumes? The whole idea that Saxo casually or systematically improved the resemblance of the two tales—a notion Elton and others also hold to be probable[26]—has no positive evidence to support it and requires a series of arbitrary assumptions about Saxo's sources and his employment of them in the *Vita Amlethi*. For some reason scholars find it difficult to accept the notion that Saxo could be familiar with the legends of a number of similar heroes—Amleth, Harald and Halfdan, Brutus—and not necessarily wish to make them more like one another.

My comparison of the Hamlet and Brutus stories disproves the view that the similarities are superficial and occasional,[27] and demonstrates rather that they are often deep and reach from the beginning through to the end. The sometimes obvious, sometimes subtle nature of the parallels, moreover, precludes explaining them by positing a simple literary transformation of Brutus to Amleth. The basic question is whether the correspondences are better explained by reference to oral development from a common ancestor or to oral development of the one from the other.

The problem is not answered by the chronology of the written texts, which provide us only with a terminus ante quem for the existence of the oral stories that inspired them. While Scandinavians presumably have had oral stories for as long a time as Romans have, the direct evidence for them is much later because Scandinavian literature came into being at a much later date. Apart from runic inscriptions, Danish literature first appears in the twelfth century, the century of Saxo's birth. The legends of Hamlet and Brutus, in their current forms, were recorded by historians of their native lands very soon after each society began investigating and writing down its traditional history. Accordingly, although the written records of the Brutus story are over one thousand years older than those of the Hamlet story, the oral story on which the Brutus texts depend is not necessarily older. How old the stories were, in these or in earlier shapes, we simply have no means of knowing.

As Jiriczek observes, it is logically easier to imagine the Brutus story as a development of the Hamlet story than the other way around, and if the two legends existed only in the forms of contemporary folktale texts, no one would doubt that Brutus developed from Hamlet.[28] There is no reason to believe that the reverse is likelier or even that it is possible, if by the Brutus legend we mean a story much like that in the texts we have. Consider the foreign-land episode. When placed side by side and their common features extracted, Amleth's journey to Britain and Brutus's trip to Delphi suggest, as we have seen, a reasonably coherent sequence of events. In the Amleth episode the connections between these events are clear, but in the Brutus tale some of the relationships are quite uncertain. What does Brutus hope to accomplish by bringing a secret gift or message to Apollo? Is there a causal relationship between Brutus's stick and the oracular message, or between his interpretation of the message and his future acquisition of rule? It is difficult to imagine how these obscurely connected features might give rise to the corresponding episode in the Amleth story, though there can be no question that the two episodes are close relatives of some kind. It is not impossible, so far as we know, for the Northern legend to be a development of an earlier form of the Brutus legend or of another branch of the Brutus story that did not find its way into ancient literature, though there is no more reason to believe that this is the case than that the Southern legend derives in a similar way from an ancestral form of the Hamlet tale. Since neither story can be understood easily as a simple offshoot of the other, at least in the forms in which we know them, it seems best to explain them as independent developments of a common ancestor, whether the hero of that story was named Brutus or Hamlet or something else.

The major conclusion to which these analyses lead is that the biography of Hamlet does not stand alone as a unique Scandinavian story but is genetically related to at least two other European historical legends and that these three legends are probably collaterals. If that is correct, the Hamlet of tradition is a regional variant of a more widely known story whose history extends back in time over a thousand years before the first literary records of the Northern hero. This story we can call the *Hero as Fool.*

What is peculiar to the Hamlet form of the story type is then not so much its substance as the particular ways in which its materials are realized, for the most important narrative ideas can also be found in the other two legends. To take one instance: the story of H and H elaborates the tension between the villain and the hero; the Brutus story does little of the sort, but it does locate the hero in the villain's own house; and the heroes of both stories play the fool at one time or another. But only in the Hamlet story are these three ideas combined, so that the dramatic possibilities of the suspicious uncle and the dissembling nephew who dwell together in the same house are exploited.

The concept of a legend type does not in itself disprove the historicity of every incident or of any particular incident in each story, but it does reveal as unlikely the historicity of each hero's traditional biography taken as a whole and does make suspect the historicity of any part, especially those parts which are common to two or more stories. It implies of course that these tales circulated and migrated as integral narratives.[29] The Hero as Fool may have spread within Europe by diffusion or descended among Indo-Europeans by inheritance from the proto-Indo-European repertoire or been transmitted by a combination of these means. The probability that the story is an old Indo-European legend would be stronger if it could be shown that a variant of the story existed in India or Iran. The likeliest candidate among the eastern Indo-Europeans is the Iranian legend of Kai Khusrau.

> Siyawish, son of King Kaus of Iran, married Farangis, daughter of King Afrasiyab of Turan. Presently, however, Afrasiyab's jealous brother Garsiwaz poisoned the Turanian king's mind

> against his son-in-law, so that Afrasiyab had Siyawish executed. Piran, the king's counselor, persuaded Afrasiyab to spare Farangis, who was with child. Piran took the widow to his house, where she gave birth to a son, Kai Khusrau. Rather than turn the boy over to the king, Piran entrusted him to shepherds to be raised. Years later he informed Afrasiyab that the boy was still alive but was an idiot. The king wanted to see for himself. Piran privately instructed Kai Khusrau to play the fool. When the king questioned the lad, his replies seemed to the monarch to be senseless, though the answers can be interpreted metaphorically as statements concerning the speaker's present weakness and intended revenge. The king sent the youth away, supposing that no harm could come from him. Later, Kai Khusrau became king of Iran, captured Afrasiyab and Garsiwaz, and put them to death.

Although the Iranian story may be genetically connected with the Hero as Fool, the parallels are not so thick as to force one to conclude that it is.

Three: Legend and Literature

It might be thought that few tasks could be more obvious than how to set down a traditional story in writing. One could simply write out what one hears, or has heard, and it would be done. But in fact such texts are very rare. Persons who have put traditional stories into writing have been as a rule less interested in recording oral storytelling than in making literature of one kind or another. Being storytellers themselves rather than students of the oral tale, or being both, they have used writing to retell rather than to reproduce. The text that is produced inevitably shows something both of its oral past and also of its new literary condition.[1] It is possible, of course, for a particular literary treatment of an oral story to be a virtual transcription that owes nothing of significance to the writer, or for it to be essentially a work of literature with little resemblance to its oral predecessor. Neither extreme, however, characterizes Saxo's narrative. For on the one hand the parallels between the *Vita Amlethi* and the *Ambales Saga*, and between the Hamlet tradition taken together and its analogues in European legendry indicate that Saxo is primarily transmitting, not inventing, a story. And on the other hand Saxo's retelling the legend in literary Latin is sufficient in itself to show that the role he adopted was more active than that of a strict transcriber of an oral tale. We may therefore pose the question: what is the relationship of the *Vita Amlethi* to the oral story of Hamlet? To what extent does

Saxo reproduce in writing the traits of live storytelling? To what extent does he introduce other techniques of narration?

As a matter of fact, the influence of the Latin literary tradition on Saxo has already been described with some thoroughness by Saxo scholars and by historians of Danish literature.[2] But of the oral narration very little has been said. The principal reason for this is that students of literature are, as is to be expected, more familiar with written texts and literary techniques than with oral legends and oral storytelling; and, after all, we know Saxo only as a writer and the *Vita Amlethi* only as a text. Consequently, although we may all allow that the plot of the Hamlet story has its origin among oral storytellers, no one has inquired whether there are not *other* features of Saxo's narration that also have their origin in oral storytelling. We find it more convenient simply to assume that the oral component, whatever exactly it may be, is of no importance for understanding the nature of Saxo's narration.

The Latin Heritage

As we have seen, it is impossible for us to form a really accurate idea of the Hamlet story as it circulated among Danes and Icelanders in Saxo's day. Even if we are correct in surmising that Saxo knew Danish as well as Icelandic versions of the story, we still do not know who his informants were or how he collated their narratives. And though it appears likely that Saxo modified some details of the received tradition, in our ignorance of his sources we cannot know how freely or conservatively he handled them. In short, an attempt to compare the content of the *Vita Amlethi* with that of its lost predecessors cannot take us very far in understanding the formation of the *Vita Amlethi*.

The case is different when we turn to Saxo's language. It is here that his influence on the *Vita Amlethi* is especially visible. His employment of the Latin language was not, of course, determined by his intention to recount the Hamlet story, for that story is merely one narrative out of many in Saxo's history. Indeed, Latin is an ill-suited medium in which to communicate the story, not because it is Latin in particular, but because it is a foreign tongue. For the Hamlet story depends greatly on the native vocabulary. The most obvious loss is the wordplay in those incidents that turn upon double entendres (sec.4). There is no way to translate the puns from Danish (or Icelandic) into Latin. But Saxo chooses to retain rather than to drop the scenes in which they occur, to the bewilderment of his readers, for whom Scandinavian puns in Latin dress are unrecognizable. His decision to narrate the untranslatable is not without parallel—one thinks of Jesus' Aramaic puns which get lost in the Greek of the New Testament[3]—but the wordplay is not for that reason any more comprehensible. A more subtle casualty is the blurring over of Danish categories. Saxo must seek substitutes for native terms such as *viking* and *jarl* and *thrall* and *hall*. The more removed in space or time the reader is from Saxo's own culture, the more the native color fades. The remote reader loses much possibility of associating the Latin words with the Danish cultural elements to which Saxo makes them refer. When François de Belleforest, retelling the *Vita Amlethi* in French, came upon Saxo's description of the eavesdropper hiding under the *stramentum* 'straw' in the queen's bedroom, he rendered the Latin word in its rare sense of "quilt" (Commentary, sec.5). As a cultured Frenchman of the sixteenth century he presumably rejected the idea—wrongly—that straw might ever be found in a Danish royal house, and so started Saxo's humble straw on its way to becoming Shakespeare's fine arras.

The reason Saxo writes in Latin is, of course, that Latin was the language of culture and learning, the international language of his day. And Latin was the language of medieval national histories as a genre, such as Bede's *Historia ecclesiastica Anglorum* and Paul the Deacon's *Historia Langobardorum*, both of which Saxo cites and which may have served him as models for his *Gesta Danorum*.[4] There was as yet no tradition of Danish vernacular literature.

Saxo modeled his Latin style after the pagan authors of the Silver Age and of late antiquity, notably Valerius Maximus, Justin, Martianus Capella, and Curtius Rufus, not after ecclesiastical writers. This choice no doubt reflects his sometimes anticlerical attitude.[5] His own heroes are warriors, not monks. The ideals he admires in a person are, not the Christian virtues, but the old heroic values of personal honor, courage, loyalty, and military prowess. If we can judge by those passages in Saxo's work that appear to be borrowed from or inspired by earlier Latin writers, his favorite author was Valerius Maximus. Although traces of twenty-six Latin authors and anonymous works have been seen in the *Gesta Danorum*, Saxo borrowed more from Valerius than from all the others combined. In all, 934 traces of Valerius's phrasing have been found distributed over 1,825 places in Saxo, whereas only 58 borrowings in 86 places have been noticed in his next most used model, Justin.[6] Valerius composed the *Facta ac dicta memorabilia*, a collection of historical exempla, in the early first century A.D. His style is markedly rhetorical. There is an unrelenting straining after effect, with forced metaphors, labored antitheses, sententious observations, exclamations of praise and of reproach, and so on. These are familiar traits of the pointed style, as it has been called, the characteristic style of Latin literature of the Silver Age, in the early years of which Valerius wrote his book. The pointed style avoids the obvious and the natural, and prefers instead the ingenious and the artificial.[7] It is mannered and given to moralizing. Saxo certainly admired this style and imitated it in his own narrative. Let me review the chief feature of his own literary style, as it appears in the *Vita Amlethi.*

Saxo tends to subjectivize the telling by interpreting it, offering a running commentary, as it were, on the events. Accordingly, Saxo praises Amleth after his revenge:

> A brave man and deserving to be remembered forever! He shrewdly played the fool and with an amazing pretense of folly kept hidden an intelligence more sublime than mortal. By his cunning he not only saved his own life but also managed to avenge his father. Because of his skillful defense of himself and his vigorous vengeance of his father, it is hard to say which is greater, his courage or his cleverness. [Sec.7]

Upon Amleth's death, Saxo again praises him, but indirectly, by a brief evaluation of his life, which assigns the cause of his early downfall to a force outside a man's control:

> If he had had as much luck as he had cleverness, he would have equaled the gods in fame and surpassed the labors of Hercules in the glory of his accomplishments. [Sec. 10]

At other times Saxo casts his comment in the form of a general truth, as though to relate a particular event in the narrative to a law of nature. After Fengi murders his brother and weds the widow, Saxo observes:

> For man who gives in to one crime rushes headlong into a second, since one goads him to the next. [Sec. 2]

And when Herminthrud faithlessly deserts her husband for his slayer, Saxo adds a string of gnomic and metaphoric comments, condemning all women for their flightiness:

> All vows of women become void with changes in fortune, are dissolved by the shifting of time, and disappear with the play of fate, for their faith stands on slippery feet. Though they are quick to promise you something, they are slow to keep it. Slaves of pleasure, they leap headfirst and gaping in their continual longing for something new, and forget the old. [Sec. 10]

Saxo's fondness of making explicit the inherent irony of an event is another debt to the pointed style. The rewritten letter carried by Amleth's two escorts is the occasion for this comment:

> When they reached Britain, the messengers went to the king and handed him the letter which they believed was the instrument of another's destruction, but really contained their own sentence of death. [Sec. 6]

And when the deceived Britons flee at the sight of Amleth's army of puppets, Saxo says:

> Terrified at the sight, the Britons fled before the fighting began, conquered by the very dead whom they had subdued when they were alive. [Sec. 9]

Perhaps no feature is more typical of Saxo's narration than his habit of repeating the same thought in two or three different ways, accumulating clauses that contain words more than content and displaying his large vocabulary and control of the Latin language, a display that was intended to delight his learned contemporaries and no doubt succeeded in doing so, but strikes the modern reader as pompous or tedious. For example:

> Even though our intentions separate us, the laws of nature bind us together, for we are united by them however much hatred keeps our minds apart. [Sec. 1]

> He justified the crime by pretending that he had acted from good will and disguised the murder as an act of duty. [Sec. 2]

> Our anger should cease after death; our feud should stop at the grave. Although there is hatred between us while we both live, we should not be so cruel as to persecute the other's dead body. [Sec. 1]

In this last passage Saxo expresses the same notion fully three times: "our anger should cease after death" = "our feud should stop at the grave" = "although there is hatred between us while we both live, we should not be so cruel as to persecute the other's dead body."

The most substantial kind of amplification is Saxo's treatment of the speeches in the story. In the classical manner he dresses up his narrative and draws it out by elaborating what the characters say to one another, occasionally at some length. Notable are Koller's chivalric reply to Ørvendil (sec. 1), Amleth's bitter reproach to his mother (sec. 5), Amleth's long oration to the Jutes (sec. 8), and Herminthrud's address to Amleth in Scotland (sec. 9). Consider for a moment Amleth's oration to the Jutes after the killing of his uncle. Saxo gives him a lengthy and elaborate speech such as a Roman rhetorician might have composed, with the antitheses of ancient rhetoric, touches of classical imagery such as the despot's *sceptrum* 'staff', and an occasional paronomasia as in '*pater*' father and '*patria*' fatherland. Northern terseness is transformed into oratorical verbosity and Roman boasting. In its portraits of Ørvendil and Fengi, the speech largely ignores the rest of the story. Here one learns for the first time that Ørvendil was a kind, just, mild, and gentle king, like a father to his people, whereas before, one was told only that he had a glorious career. Fengi is here not simply the murderer of his brother but also a despot of the very worst sort as well as a man who delighted in crime as a matter of policy. He killed his brother, not from envy at his success (as Saxo informed us at the time) nor to protect Geruth (as Fengi himself alleged after the event), but because he wanted to enslave his countrymen and fill the land with crime. Amleth is not made here to reply, as he might have done, to Fengi's pretext for the killing, but speaks instead of character traits, motives, and actions that are found only in this speech. The oration is a virtually independent composition, rhetorically elaborated for its own interest rather than for its relevance to its context.

Saxo puts his Scandinavian materials through a Roman sieve, narrating his account of Hamlet's career (and of Danish history in general) the way he imagined a Roman historian of the Silver Age might do it. His style has the superficial appearance of being interpretative and therefore weighty, but its thought is thoroughly shallow, and its devices are really aesthetic rather than philosophic. What Saxo adds is, not substance or feeling or insight into the story and its characters, but a series of pointed effects that in combination with a receptive reader will enhance the enjoyment of the narration by calling attention to the telling itself, but in combination with a nonreceptive reader, as most readers today are likely to be, will just as certainly irritate or bore. All in all, Saxo's narration greatly slows down the pace of the oral tale. The tautology retards the progress of the action, which is now and again punctuated and brought to a temporary halt by the author's evaluative or meditative comments on the events and by the speeches that the characters pause to make.

The result does not always make for easy reading. Most Danish readers were probably more attracted to modest histories composed in simpler Latin or eventually in the vernacular than they were to Saxo's monumental work written in the classical language. An indication of readers' attitudes is provided by the appearance in Jutland in the fourteenth century of the so-called *Compendium Saxonis,* a summary of Saxo's history.[8] According to its author, Saxo's work is wordy and full of ornament and his style is difficult; consequently, he himself will turn the most notable deeds described by Saxo into plain words. In brief, he promises to translate Saxo into ordinary medieval Latin.

Saxo adopted in place of his native Danish a non-Scandinavian literary language, and with it a way of telling a story, which he substituted for the relatively direct and unmannered Northern style of oral storytelling. The narrative devices he borrowed from the Latin tradition are a display of ornaments, and they have this in common, that they all operate on the surface of the narration. None of them regularly affects what happens in the story (that is, the plot) or how it happens (what I shall here call form, for want of a more inclusive term), but only the manner in which these elements are verbalized and elaborated.[9] The plot of the story comes, as we have seen, from contemporary oral tradition. Where then does the form come from? What gives the received events their shape? From the scholarly silence on this subject, one may conclude that it is generally and implicitly assumed that the form of the action owes nothing of significance either to the literary tradition, in the sense that Saxo's Latin style does, or to the oral tradition, in the way that the Hamlet story itself does, but is in some way natural and even inevitable, and so does not attract comment. But the form of the action is not inevitable (I take it as axiomatic that narrative form is no more inevitable than narrative style is), and the thesis I shall argue is that this aspect of the *Vita Amlethi* is borrowed with little or no change from live storytelling.

The Oral Influence

Although oral storytelling varies with the individual teller's competence and with the different styles of raconteurs and regions and with other variables, oral stories from different narrators and places and times characteristically share a number of formal features. Some of these have been studied, or at least described.[10] Although it would be too much to say that they are fully understood, some of them certainly are determined by the circumstances of live storytelling. The spoken word makes special demands upon the minds of the senders and the receivers of the narrative. A teller composes, or recomposes, his story before his audience rather than in the solitude of his study; consequently, he has less occasion to ponder, correct, and refine than a writer has. And his stories are those that can be stored in their essentials in his mind, for unlike an author he must carry his stories around with him. A competent storyteller understands that his narrative can be as plain or as intricate as his talents permit, but he may lose his listeners if they cannot follow his story. Listeners, for their part, cannot set their own pace, pause at length to reflect, or return to an earlier point in the narrative, as a reader can. Since they operate constantly in the present moment, it is important that each incident, as it is told, be capable of being understood and enjoyed for itself.

Most of Saxo's narrative is resolved into little scenes or episodes, which succeed one another in narration and in chronology, as in traditional oral stories generally.[11] Each episode tells of an important or amusing event in the life of the hero and then proceeds with little transition to another such episode. Within each episode the emphasis, as in most oral stories,[12] is on action. Though Saxo frequently lets one know what is going on inside the heads of the characters, the course of the story is so dependent upon incident that the events would remain comprehensible if all notices of motive and deliberation were absent.

The action is presented in as plain a fashion as possible. It would often be difficult to simplify it further and still tell the story. A scene presents at most two active characters. In the first scene Ørvendil and Koller encounter each other while their men are elsewhere, and other scenes bring together at different times Fengi and his conniving friend, Amleth and the eavesdropper, Amleth and his mother, Amleth and the king of Britain, the king and his steward, Amleth and Herminthrud, and so on. This reflects what is probably the single most important feature of the structuring of scenes in oral stories: that no more than two characters are active at a particular time.[13]

If more than two characters are present in a scene, Saxo may treat all but one of them as though they were a single character, a procedure he shares with oral narrators.[14] The other characters become a mass character, all acting alike. Thus the miscellaneous henchmen and friends of Fengi usually act as undifferentiated bystanders. They question Amleth as a group, and as a group they laugh at his replies. When, in Britain, Amleth spurns the royal banquet, all others present—the king, the queen, Amleth's companions, and the other feasters—respond as one. While Amleth's two companions later question him in their room about his curious behavior, the two companions could well be a single person.

There is a second device in the *Vita Amlethi* and in oral narration for handling a third or fourth character in a scene. The excess characters simply become inactive, as if they were not there.[15] When Amleth is escorted into the woods to be tested for his sexual response (sec.4), the active characters are Amleth and his undifferentiated escorts. Then the group splits up: the escorts retire to the entirely inactive background so that Amleth may then turn his attentions to the woman sent to seduce him. The scene subsequently shifts away from Amleth and the girl, moving to a single one of the escorts, Amleth's foster brother, after which the narrator returns again to the lovers. Similarly, in the following episode in Geruth's room (sec.5), two characters are present when Amleth enters: the hidden eavesdropper and the queen. Geruth is totally ignored while the narration focuses exclusively upon the hero and the spy; once he is disposed of, but not before, Geruth is allowed to respond to her son's apparently demented behavior, and Amleth can address his mother. In the scene in which Amleth and his two companions converse in their quarters after the royal meal in Britain (sec.6), there is again a hidden eavesdropper present. He remains inactive as a character until after the conversation, when he reports what he heard to the king.[16]

On the whole, then, the dominant form of interpersonal activity is dyadic. Characters interact with each other in series of pairs. Since the characters in the legend are at almost every point polarized into two opposing groups, interactions involve two allies or two opponents. Consequently, scenes tend to dramatize either conspiracy (for example, Fengi and his friend, Amleth and Geruth, Amleth and Herminthrud, Amleth and his British wife) or conflict (Ørvendil and Koller, Amleth and the eavesdropper, Amleth and the king of Britain).[17]

Episodes in Saxo's narrative have more independence than episodes in much literary narrative, especially in literature that has been composed under the stern ideal of organic unity. The same is true of oral story in general.[18] The reason presumably is that teller and auditor have less opportunity to pause to relate one episode to another or to the whole than writer and reader do. They are of necessity much more committed to the immediacy of each present scene. The tendency to structure episodes as more nearly self-contained units, which I call episodic composition, has several important consequences for Saxo's *Vita Amlethi.*

The independence of an episode is such that the events may be referred to nowhere else in the text and may themselves contain few or no external references. Saxo thus may make less effort to prepare for a forthcoming scene well in advance of the scene or to follow up its implications so fully as a writer in a strictly literary tradition may. Like an oral storyteller, he frequently introduces the necessary elements within the episode itself, simplifying both the telling and the appreciation of the episode by minimizing its dependence upon information that would otherwise have to be implanted earlier and recalled later. So we first learn of Amleth's foster brother and foster sister in the episode in which the two characters appear (sec.4). A narrator who composed less episodically might have introduced them earlier. Similarly, Saxo mentions the pact of Fengi and the British king long after the two characters themselves have entered the story, because the precise nature of their relationship is important only in the episode in which the British king must be motivated to act against his son-in-law (sec.9). It is then that we are informed of it.

The converse of this is that when something is no longer needed in the story, it may be dropped with little or no explanation. A character who has played his role is silently dismissed, dead or alive, from the story; an object that has done its work is forgotten. This phenomenon is familiar from oral story.[19] After the episode of the test in the woods (sec.4), Amleth's foster brother, so important an ally in the adventure, ceases to exist for the story. Nor is Amleth's foster sister, an equally helpful ally, ever mentioned again. Later, after Amleth returns to Jutland from his victory in Britain, accompanied by his two wives (sec.9), we hear no more of his British spouse. She as well as her son are instantly forgotten because they have no further role to play in the story: Saxo is now interested only in Amleth and Herminthrud (sec.10). The fate of even so important a character as Geruth is unexplained at the end, so that we are left to guess how she fares. In oral story the role is generally more important than the character who plays it, so that when an actor is irrelevant to the plot, he is neglected; when needed, he is at hand. It is the same with objects. After Amleth's gold-filled sticks have done their work (sec.6), one never again hears of them.[20]

By these means a story gains in immediacy. Teller and listener deal with what is immediately relevant and only so long as it remains so. A more serious consequence of episodic composition, at least for the reflective reader of the *Vita Amlethi*, is its tolerance of inconsistency. Saxo's narrative expresses predominantly the old heroic ethos, but it contains as well elements that did not arise in heroic legend and are not fully assimilated to it. The legend shows the influence of other narrative genres—folktale and romance. When the legend remains true to the folktales it has adopted, its realistic atmosphere yields for the while to an atmosphere of supranormal mystery or of benevolent chance. The episode of the feast in the hall of the British king is a variant, as we shall see (Commentary, sec.6), of an international folktale in which the hero possesses extraordinarily keen perception, an ability that Amleth therefore exhibits in the banquet scene but nowhere else in the legend. Since Amleth's means of deduction there are not all accounted for by natural means, the episode gives the impression that his powers go beyond the natural in this respect. An air of mystery about the nature of the hero is created that neither recurs nor receives explanation in the rest of the legend. One is temporarily in a different narrative universe.

The other adopted folktale (Commentary, sec.9) illustrates clearly the difference between a variant of a tale that has been assimilated to the dominant ethos of the legend and one that has not. Fearing that a certain lad is destined to become his son-in-law, a king sends the young man to the palace carrying a letter to the queen, which instructs her to put the bearer to death. On the way the hero falls asleep, and the letter is read by another, either the princess, who falls in love with him, or a band of robbers or the like, who feel compassion for him. The sympathetic person substitutes for the king's letter another letter that instructs the queen to wed the bearer to the princess, and so it happens. Both forms of the tale appear in the *Vita Amlethi*, each of them deviating in certain ways from the ordinary oral variants.

In the first instance (sec.6), Amleth's companions bear a runic letter from King Fengi to the king of Britain, bidding the latter put the youth to death. During the voyage, when the hero's two companions are sleeping, Amleth prudently searches for the letter, learns its contents, and makes the usual subsititution, adding that his companions should be put to death. In the second instance (sec.9), the British king sends Amleth off to Scotland with a letter asking for the hand of the Scots queen in marriage to the king, who in reality expects that the queen, according to her custom, will put the suitor to death. Close to the queen's residence Amleth naps, during which time one of the queen's scouts brings both his letter and his illustrated shield to the queen. Greatly impressed, she changes the letter so that it sues for her hand on behalf of Amleth himself. As before, Amleth weds the woman and later kills the man who sent him.

Despite their being examples of the same folktale type, the two tellings belong to different worlds. In the former the change from folktale to heroic legend was efficiently made. The role of the letter-bearer was neatly transferred from the hero to Fengi's housecarls. Fengi could not trust Amleth to be so unsuspecting as the hero of the folktale, so it was natural for the king's henchmen to control the letter. That in turn allowed Amleth to play the role of the sympathetic rewriter of the letter, acting, however, on his own behalf rather than for the sleeping letter-carriers. Amleth takes charge of his own destiny, leaving nothing to chance.

It was perhaps impossible for the second variant to use the same twist while also maintaining its identity as a separate adventure. In any event it retains the spirit of the folktale. Amleth undertakes a dangerous mission for his father-in-law, a mission whose nature he presumably understands, although he does not appreciate the hostile motive of the sender. Setting out for Scotland without any plan, he trusts wholly in his luck. Near the queen's estate he rests in a meadow and is saved from death by the good fortune that a Scots scout is able to steal and replace the letter he carries and that the usually hostile queen instantly desires him in marriage. The hero who elsewhere tries in every way to influence his destiny is temporarily transformed into one who passively lets destiny work its will upon him. The chess-player briefly becomes a pawn.

Other discordant elements arise from the mixing of the older heroic ethos with the more recent taste for romance, each dominating different parts of the legend. The romantic ethos appears in several forms. It first occurs in the holmgang of Ørvendil and Koller, where it is expressed in the chivalry, rather than simple honor, of the duelers. They agree before the fight that an injured man shall receive compensation from the other for the harm he sustains. The usual practice was just the reverse of this. An injured man might have the right to pay an agreed sum to his opponent to ransom his life (Commentary, sec. 1). In the same episode Saxo lyrically describes the beauties of the island's vegetation. The purpose of introducing the description is to motivate the two vikings to wander inland so that they may chance to meet each other alone. The theme of attractive nature reappears later as a device to motivate Amleth to take a nap in a wayside meadow (sec. 9). Whether the inspiration for these instances of the characters' aesthetic response to nature was the oral ballad, classical literature, or some other influence, they show a relationship between character and environment that expresses new interests and emphases, for descriptions of the landscape and of the characters' appreciation of it are foreign to heroic story in the North.[21] Finally, suggestions of romantic love make an appearance in the dealings of Amleth and his wives (secs. 9–10).

In sum, the legend here and there has given way to newer fashion in story, assigning to its characters an exaggerated concern (from the viewpoint of the heroic ethos) for each other in the form of chivalry or of romantic love, and for their environment in the form of an aesthetic response to nature;[22] and it has adopted without complete assimilation episodes from folktales in which a character possesses mysterious powers or is the darling of fate, passively benefiting from a world of benevolent chance. The point is that neither Saxo nor the narrators who preceded him have unified these rather independent narrative parts into a consistent whole, so the story wavers between the heroic, the romantic, and the fantastic. The sensitive reader may feel that he is, not in one narrative world, but in several at different times. Of course, an assessment of the effect of the parts should be made not only from the viewpoint of literary values but also from the standpoint of oral storytelling. Readers dealing with orally inspired literature have a habit of putting together things that listeners perceive separately.[23] Accustomed to episodic composition and to the role of the auditor, the listener is inclined to take things as they come. Teller and hearer, being less concerned or able to relate each episode to the narrrative whole or to demand consistency so strongly as the author and his reader ordinarily do, are more tolerant of disharmonies among the parts of the narrative.

Saxo's portrayal of the characters appears to aim for clarity and simple effect. The attributes of each character are few, as is ordinarily the case for traditional characters.[24] Thus Amleth is cunning and honorable, Fengi is cunning and dishonorable, the foster sister is loyal, and so forth. For what is important about the characters personally is their abilities and their adherence to or deviation from certain social ideals. In the contention of Amleth and Fengi, both men are cunning, though Amleth is more successfully so; what distinguishes their character is Amleth's sense of honor and Fengi's lack of it.

There is no development of character, which also is the usual lot of traditional characters.[25] Amleth's and Fengi's fortunes rise and fall, but their dominant traits are with them to the end. Geruth is possibly an exception to this rule, since her behavior changes significantly for the better after she is reproached by her son (sec. 5), or so Amleth at least might assess it. However, one might argue that she does not really change but is consistently passive, yielding in succession to the will of the men in her life—first her father Rørik, then Ørvendil, then Fengi, then Amleth; later on she is the victim of Viglek (sec. 10).

Saxo never describes the natural physical appearance of the characters or their customary habits of dress. Oral narrators rarely do.[26] He mentions only changes in appearance, and then only when they are connected with the plot, as when Amleth adopts the guise of a fool or when he has a special shield made for himself. The attributes of the characters are expressed primarily through their actions, the usual procedure in traditional oral story.[27] Although Saxo frequently reveals what a character thinks or feels, he always tells what he does. Character is simply a function of role. Whatever Amleth is—heroic or romantic or brilliantly perceptive—at any particular point in the narrative depends upon the action demanded of him by the episode itself. Although the reader may sense a certain depth and complexity in the hero's character, the intuition would not be wholly accurate since it would depend upon a synchronic overview of the story more than upon a view that focusses upon the episodes successively.

Overall, Saxo's characterization tends to be clear and simple. Every attempt is made to keep the individualized characters few, clearly outlined, and distinct from one another so that the significance of their interactions may be clearly grasped. Two characters who share a similar position or are otherwise closely linked may either not be individualized at all or be sharply distinguished by being portrayed as opposite types. The two men who escort Amleth to Britain (sec. 6) are an example of the former case. They are not distinguished from each other. The second case is exemplified by the two brothers who jointly rule Jutland (secs. 1–2). Ørvendil might be a model of all that a man of high birth and office should be if he wished to win his peers' approbation. He sets out to increase his wealth and renown by roving as a viking chieftain, advertising his courage in battle and enriching himself by plunder. In three years he is a famous man in the North. He overcomes the king of Norway in a bold duel. He follows up his military and financial success with great marital success, gaining the hand of King Rørik's daughter Geruth. He is a chieftain at the height of glory, the manly ideal of a heroic society. Fengi's only notable act is to envy his brother's good fortune. And when Fengi does takes action, it is the action of a sneak. Ørvendil's honorableness, illustrated by his keeping his bargain with the Norwegian king, though no man would have known it if he had not, is in sharp contrast to Fengi's behavior after the slaying of his brother, for though he acknowledges the killing, he dishonestly alleges noble reasons for the ignoble act. Fengi is passive and indirect; Ørvendil is active and direct. Similarly, of Amleth's two wives, one is passive and loyal; the other, aggressive and disloyal. This inclination to assimilate to each other two characters in similar roles or to distinguish them by sharp contrast is a familiar technique of the oral storyteller.[28]

The action of the *Vita Amlethi* is closely grouped about a protagonist, as in most traditional narrative.[29] Once Amleth comes on the scene, he figures in every episode. Virtually all other characters are in a relationship of ally or adversary to him, so that at every point in the story the members of the militant cast belong to one or the other of two camps. Whereas Amleth plays the protagonist throughout, the role of the antagonist is taken by Fengi, the British king, and Viglek, who adopt it in succession as though one relayed it to the next. This dyadic polarization on the level of the story differs little from the dyadic polarization on the level of the scene. Both represent interaction reduced to its simplest number. Virtually everything that does not concern the protagonist or his current antagonist is excluded from the legend.

Saxo begins his story at the beginning, not in medias res, and proceeds chronologically to its conclusion. Its plot is single-stranded: flashbacks and digressions, except for a few explanatory sentences, are avoided, and no secondary stories with secondary protagonists are worked into the narrative. This is the standard method of traditional oral story.[30] Apart from the occasions in which time is suspended in order that the teller may comment on the action or describe a condition, the story moves unflinchingly forward. For an aural audience listening to a story of action, this is the simplest and probably most effective procedure.

Like an oral narrator, Saxo prefers for each of the events of his story to take place one after the other, in succession, rather than for two events to occur at the same time.[31] He rarely attempts to coordinate significant actions that occur simultaneously in different places. Thus, though Ørvendil and Koller are enticed to stroll inland from different locations at the same time (sec. 1), their actions are uniform and identical and therefore easy to envision. When simultaneous but different activities are carried out by characters in different places, Saxo's method is to analyze the activity into action and uniform process. Characters in different places are never simultaneously engaged in complex action; if both are active, only one of them is involved in a complex action. The narrator attends to the action until he has it pass into uniform process, and then he springs from it to the other scene. This technique for handling simultaneous events in Homeric oral poetry has been called the *analyzing-and-leaping method*.[32] When Amleth's escorts leave him alone with the girl in the woods (sec.4), characters are located in two or three different places. While the observers observe (= uniform process) and Amleth and the girl confront each other (= uniform process), the foster brother devises, fashions, and sends a secret message to Amleth (= complex action). While he is doing this, we are to assume that the observers and the observed continue without significant change the activity in which they were engaged when they were last mentioned. Then we leave the foster brother and follow the gadfly back to Amleth, who decodes and acts on the message (= complex action.) Once he eludes his companions, they cease to be relevant, so that we return to the more usual narrative situation, which is activity in a single place. Another example: when Amleth nears Herminthrud's dwelling (sec.9), the narrator wishes to represent activity occurring simultaneously in the queen's estate and in the nearby meadow. Amleth posts sentries and goes to sleep in the meadow. While the guards guard and their leader naps (= uniform process), the queen dispatches scouts to spy on the foreigners (= complex action). Back now at the meadow, a scout steals the letter and shield (= complex action), while the queen awaits her men in her house (= uniform process). Leaving Amleth and his men still guarding and sleeping (= uniform process), we spring back to the royal hall, where the patient queen reads and modifies the letter (= complex action). Then we return to Amleth, who awakens and joins the waiting queen in her hall (= complex action).

Since narrative is a linear medium, there is no way for a narrator really to present two complex events at the same time. The analyzing-and-leaping method is probably the technique most commonly used in oral narrative for representing simultaneous events, though no one has yet studied the subject generally. The method is in harmony with the oral storyteller's habit of moving his story constantly forward, for if he related first one complex action and then a second, simultaneous complex action, part of his story would come to a halt while he regressed in time to pick up the other part. Saxo's method is also congruent with the point of view commonly adopted by the oral raconteur, that of reporting more or less what a single observer might have seen and heard in each place. But simple succession is employed far more than synchronism.

Saxo treats the physical world very simply. Except for a couple of instances (secs. 1, 9) in which the natural pleasantness of a place is used to explain a character's actions, the setting has no interest for him beyond its function as a backdrop and stage for the actors. Whether nature or king's estate, it is named but not described. In the same way he largely ignores cultural peculiarities, as a traditional narrator is also likely to do when the matter is not relevant to the plot. Thus, in spite of the fact that the action of the *Vita Amlethi* takes place in Denmark, Britain, and Scotland, Saxo mentions nothing exotic in the two non-Scandinavian lands. In all ways the three kingdoms are treated as culturally homogeneous, since cultural peculiarities are irrelevant to his story. Danish ways are projected onto Britons and Scots. As in nearly all folk narrative, the complication of foreign languages is passed over without comment. It is a little world of universal familiarity, and Amleth could as well be traveling next door as to another country. The only gesture towards creating a non-Danish atmosphere outside of Denmark is the assigning of a German name to the Scots queen. Danish ballads often drew upon the name pool of neighboring Germany for foreign names.[33] We are expected to hear the name *Herminthrud*, not as German, but simply as foreign.

The choice of Britain and Scotland is, however, not wholly arbitrary. It the teller had wanted Amleth dispatched to a hostile land, he might have sent him south to the Saxons; if he had wished him to go to a land of sorcerers, he would have sent him east to the Finns. Britain and Scotland are free of these extraneous associations, and their employment probably reflects the many friendly and hostile connections between Scandinavia and the British Isles that had been established in the centuries preceding Saxo. These old ties are remembered in Danish folktales even today, in which the hero's quest land, if named, is still most often England.[34] But on the whole Saxo makes virtually no effort to portray foreign lands as being really different from Denmark. Like other elements of the background, they are not interesting for their own sake.

Although this list of narrative traits could be extended, these are probably the most significant formal features, other than the plot itself, that Saxo's composition has in common with purely oral compositions. It is evident that, just as the style of the *Vita Amlethi* is mostly Latinate and literary, its narrative form is essentially oral. It is, moreover, no exaggeration to say that one cannot appreciate the construction of many scenes in the *Vita Amlethi* without understanding something of their oral form—the limit of two active characters at a time; episodic composition, with its strong emphasis on the present moment, resulting in somewhat independently structured episodes, with characters and objects remembered or forgotten according to the convenience of the plot, and with uneven characterization of the hero and his world owing to the semiautonomous use of materials; the preference for dealing with one thing at a time, reflected in the dislike of synchrony; the mostly static characters, possessing few essential traits and displaying little external appearance or inner reality; the lack of description of the external world and, in general, of anything that is not directly related to concrete action, to which all else in the story is subordinate.

Saxo's own practice implies that either intuitively or consciously he himself isolated style and form as narrative elements and consistently distinguished the two. For in connection with the former he feels quite at liberty to do as he pleases. He discards the inherited oral style and replaces it with an alien style, employing a literary diction, lengthening the speeches, subjectivizing the story, and so on. But with the latter he carefully keeps intact the oral structure of the action and permits himself to change nothing in kind. Saxo's procedure in fact reflects that which at all times has been the most common way of giving literary treatment to traditional stories. It has been the usual, though not invariable, method from Herodotos to the present day. One could call these texts *light treatments*. The writers characteristically conserve the inherited plot and form, which they evidently take to represent the true essence of the tale, but treat freely the way in which the apparently essential elements are recounted. *Heavy treatments*, in which the traditional form is significantly altered or altogether rejected, are certainly rarer. I shall consider this procedure in Part 4.

Saxo as Narrator

Let us examine in detail a sample of Saxo's narration in order to illustrate the interaction of literary style with oral form. I select part of the bedroom episode (sec. 5). Saxo's narration is far from being uniform and consistent throughout. In the portions of the passage in which speech is reported, we find rhetoric and repetition. Elements are burdened with considerable ornament, producing a slower pace and a more noticeable contrast and even incongruity between the rather direct plot on the one hand and the extreme artifice of telling on the other hand. At the other end are the narrative portions, in which Saxo is as economic with his information as in the dramatic portions he is redundant. Here he is rapid and summary, sometimes overly so, with the result that we can even be inadequately informed about the nature of the situation and would cherish an additional sentence or two. Saxo does not entirely set aside his artifice here, but it is mostly restricted to nonaction narrative. Thus he uses antitheses to introduce Fengi's friend (the man, Saxo says, had more confidence than judgment), to close the incident (the man was as ready to execute as to invent a plan), and to close the bedroom scene (the queen discovered that an old passion was preferable to a present pleasure). It is when he describes concrete action that he is plainest and probably closest to the style of a Danish oral raconteur. Saxo does not use the pointed style so consistently as he uses the oral form.

He much prefers the foreground. The principal actions are clearer than their temporal and local contexts or features of the background. Thus we understand what Amleth does to the eavesdropper, but not exactly when he does it or where he is at each moment or how he gets away with it all. Similarly, we can follow the essentials of the interaction of Amleth and Geruth but not how the situation was set up. Saxo typically selects for the crucial actions that constitute the logical chain of events and omits the circumstantial details of ordinary reality. Here is the passage:

> Everyone was worsted and unable to open the hidden lock of the young man's cleverness.

This summary observation forms the transition to the incident. A single thought is expressed in two ways, the one more prosaic, the other more poetic: "Everyone was worsted" = (everyone) "was unable to open the hidden lock of the young man's cleverness."

> But a certain one of Fengi's friends . . .

Polonius's prototype is given no name either now or later in the text, nor is his office or his relationship to Fengi specified in greater detail.[35]

> . . . who had more confidence than he had judgment . . .

The king's friend is characterized with a rhetorical antithesis between the apparent and the real, suggesting, in this case, that he will fail in what he undertakes.

> . . . said that no ordinary trap would expose Amleth's intricate cunning; he was too obstinate to be reached by trivial efforts, and so it was useless to pit a simple test against his complex cunning.

Introducing his plan, the man states the same notion thrice: "no ordinary trap would expose Amleth's intricate cunning" = "he was too obstinate to be reached by trivial efforts" = "it was useless to pit a simple test against his complex cunning." To whom is Fengi's friend addressing his observations? Presumably to Fengi. Where is this meeting taking place? Perhaps in the royal hall, but the location is unimportant and so is not specified. The interval of time between the previous episode and this is likewise left unspecified, and for the same reason. The narrator is interested only in the speech.

> Thinking the matter through, he said, he had hit upon a subtler way, one which would not be hard to put into effect and would without a doubt lead them to learn what they wanted to know. Fengi was to pretend some important business and purposely make a show of departure. Amleth was to be enclosed alone with his mother in her bedroom, but before that it should be arranged for a man to station himself, unknown to the two of them, in a dark part of the room to overhear carefully what they should talk about . . .

The man relates the plan itself with an economy of expression. Unfortunately, it is not matched by a fullness of necessary detail. Just what is his subtle plan anyway? Why must Fengi leave the place? How is the closeting of Amleth and the queen to be managed?

> ... for if her son was at all sane, he would not hesitate to speak out to his own mother, and would not be afraid to confide in the very woman who gave him birth.

Fengi's anonymous friend cannot resist concluding his plan with the flourish of a geminated thought. The speaker's economy of essential detail is thus succeeded by a liberal expenditure of the obvious.

> He himself eagerly volunteered to play the spy to show that he was just as ready to carry out a plan as to devise it.

Saxo casts the man's motive in the form of a stock rhetorical opposition between word and deed.

> Pleased by the idea, Fengi made a pretense of a long journey and departed.

Our assumption that Fengi was party to the conversation is thus confirmed. Saxo's reference to his departure indicates that the conspiratorial conversation has ended. Saxo does not ease us out of the meeting; when the last necessary element has been mentioned, the incident is simply over. The actual details of the plan remain vague. The king makes an unspecified excuse and leaves for an unspecified destination. Without further transition the eavesdropper is said to go to work.

> The man who had proposed the plan went secretly to the room in which Amleth was being enclosed with his mother ...

From the description of the plan narrated above, we know at least that the site of the test was to be the queen's bedroom, but we still do not know how it was arranged for Amleth and Geruth to be enclosed in the room. The mechanics of the plot remain less clear than its purpose.

> ... and concealed himself under the straw.

Saxo assumes his readers will know what straw is doing in the queen's bedroom and does not elaborate upon its presence.

> But Amleth had a remedy for the trap.

So Amleth is now present. When did he enter? Is Geruth also in the room yet? We are not informed. Saxo has passed over these details, continuing his narrative with the next important element, Amleth's response to the situation.

> Fearing that someone might secretly eavesdrop, he . . .

Why should Amleth just now fear an eavesdropper? Our understanding of the scene is limited by our inadequate information concerning how the closeting was set up. Without this knowledge we cannot be sure what information it was supposed the hero had at his disposal.

> . . . resorted at first to his usual silliness, crowing like a noisy rooster and beating his arms together as though he were flapping wings. Getting up on the straw, he began to leap all around to find out whether anything lay lurking there. When he perceived a lump beneath his feet, he clove the spot with his sword, stabbing the man who lay underneath, dragged him out of his hiding place and slew him.

Saxo reports this simply, since it is a series of concrete actions, and also adequately. Since the action involves the searching hero and the lurking spy, the queen's presence and her response to her son's behavior are out of the narrator's range. As the third character in the scene, she is inactive.

> He cut up the body . . .

Does Amleth do his butchering in Geruth's room?

> . . . cooked the pieces in boiling water . . .

The locale has obviously changed, but where are we now? Saxo skips over the fact of Amleth's exodus and focuses on the disposal of the body, narrating only that information which is necessary for following the logic of the story.

> . . . and dumped them through the hole of the outhouse for the swine to eat, strewing the putrid refuse with the wretch's limbs.

As with the straw, Saxo assumes that his readers will understand this feature of a Danish royal estate, and elaborates no further. Now that Amleth has disposed of the spy, we are entitled to wonder what the other inhabitants of the place think about his antisocial behavior. Will they not naturally take the opportunity to become active characters now in order to protest the slaughter of the king's friend? Not at all, as it turns out. But can they not see what Amleth has done? Apparently not. But if not, why not? Saxo does not explain.

> Having in this way foiled the plot, he went back to the room.

In a rare acknowledgement of the ordinary mechanics of the action, Saxo reports Amleth's reentry.

> When his mother cried out and began to weep for the folly of her son to his face . . .

Now that the eavesdropper is gone, Geruth replaces him as the other active character in the scene so that for the first time her presence and response are mentioned. A narrator could have focused on her feelings during Amleth's absence with the corpse, but Saxo does not, since it would be uneconomical, contributing nothing to the advancement of the plot, and would involve a synchrony. Accordingly, Amleth's return is Geruth's cue to respond now to his earlier behavior in the way she would have done if she had been permitted to do so at the time.

> . . . he said: "Shameless woman, why do you try to conceal your immense crime with false tears? You revel like a whore in this abominable marriage of yours . . .

The simile ("scorti more") and the adjectives signal the reappearance of a more ornate diction for the speech.

> . . . and filthily caressing and fawning upon the man who slew the father of your son.

And the present clause repeats in different words the substance of the last.

> So do mares couple with those who have overcome their mates.

The initial comparison of Geruth to a whore is now followed by another, in which she is likened to a mare.

> That is how animals behave, pairing with one after another.

The second version of the thought.

> By your actions you show that you have wholly forgotten your former husband.
> As for me . . .

This generalization on Geruth's behavior following the murder of her husband concludes Amleth's critique of her. He turns now to his own behavior.

> . . . I do not play the fool for nothing, because I do not doubt that the man who murdered his own brother would rage just as viciously against his other kin.

He explains and justifies his strategy to her.

> It is better for me to play the fool than to reveal my intentions . . .

Another version of the same thought.

> . . . and by acting the complete simpleton to guard my life.

A third version. Saxo's phrasing here ("praesidium ab extrema deliramentorum specie mutuari") may be influenced by Valerius (*Memorable Sayings and Deeds* 7. 4. 3: "praesidium ab astutia mutuantis").

> But in my mind the eagerness to avenge my father remains, and I am waiting for the right setting and the fitting time.

It is in relation to Ørvendil that Amleth finds the crucial difference between himself and his mother: Amleth remembers him while Geruth has forgotten him.

> There is a place for each thing. Against a dark and harsh mind one must use guile.

He gives two reasons, expressed as general truths, why he has not yet attempted revenge. Both elaborate upon and so to some extent repeat the thought of the preceding sentence.

> But it is a waste of time to cry for my madness when you should be lamenting your own disgrace.

Now Amleth turns back to Geruth and makes explicit the irony of her behavior in relation to his own.

> Weep not for the flaw in another's mind, but for that in your own.

Version two.

> As for the rest, keep this all to yourself." With these reproaches he wounded his mother . . .

Valerius 4.7.3 ("posteritatis convicio lacerandus") and 4.4.11 ("diuturnis conviciis laceramus") probably inspired Saxo's phrase ("Tali convicio laceratam").

> . . . and brought her back to leading a life of honor . . .

Saxo's clause ("ad excolendum virtutis habitum revocavit") appears to be inspired by Valerius 4.1. *ex.* 4 ("in pristinum habitum revocavit").

> . . . showing her that her former passion was better than her current delights.

The antithesis closes Saxo's report of the effect of Amleth's words upon his mother. The comment also concludes the scene, as it turns out, for with no further transition Saxo proceeds to report the return of Fengi and his search for the eavesdropper.

Four:
The Shakespearean Transformation

First printed in Paris in 1514, Saxo's work was well received by the learned humanists of the time and went through two more editions in the same century.[1] His *Vita Amlethi* was soon retold in French by François de Belleforest in the fifth volume of his *Histoires tragiques* (1570), a popular collection of tragic tales that went through numerous editions in the late sixteenth and early seventeenth centuries.[2] Greatly admiring precisely those features which the Danish historian had contributed to the narration, and using some of the same devices, the Frenchman actually managed to double the length of his source. But if Saxo's embellishments are sometimes tiresome, Belleforest's elaborations of Saxo's embellishments can at times test the modern reader's very ability to endure. Belleforest's retelling of the Hamlet story is as much a light treatment as Saxo's is. He largely respects the inherited form and expends most of his considerable energy on further elaborating the telling of the story. That is not to say that his prolixity or the little changes of detail he introduced here and there were without significance for the subsequent literary development of the Hamlet story, for it is in Belleforest that we first read of the late king's shade ("les ombres de Horvvendille") and of the hero's melancholy, to mention two of his seminal additions.[3] But these modifications, some of them due to Belleforest's not understanding or misunderstanding his source, are only just that: seminal; they become important for the story and really interesting only when they are further developed, as we find them in Shakespeare's drama. On the whole Belleforest is content to retell Saxo's story with no radical revisions of plot or form.

By 1589 there seems to have been a *Hamlet* on the London stage. This play, conventionally known as the *Ur-Hamlet*, is usually thought to be the work of Thomas Kyd. It was never published and has not survived. Shakespeare's company evidently purchased the play and performed it for a time. Around 1600 Shakespeare reworked it for the Chamberlain's Men, the company to which he belonged.[4] Since Shakespeare's *Tragicall Historie of Hamlet, Prince of Denmarke* shows some details that appear in Belleforest but not in Saxo, one can infer that at least one of the playwrights drew upon Belleforest's French retelling. Saxo's book was familiar to Elizabethan and Jacobean England and so could have been consulted by Shakespeare or his predecessor, but there seems to be no evidence requiring us to believe that it was.[5] Most likely, then, Shakespeare's *Hamlet* is a revision of a dramatic treatment (*Ur-Hamlet*) of a retelling (Belleforest) of a literary treatment (Saxo) of a Scandinavian legend.

The original playwright found in Belleforest's revenge story many features that were currently fashionable on the English tragic stage. The narrative offered murder and revenge, adultery and incest,[6] rhetoric and moralizing, and much else to attract an English playwright in search of suitable material. Moreover, since the French retelling largely preserved the oral form of the legend, it was structured for the most part as a succession of discrete, easily visualized incidents, reported in chronological order, and so was congenial to rehandling as a drama. Concerning this *Ur-Hamlet* we know from contemporary references that it was a tragedy, its protagonist was named Hamlet, and among its characters was a pale ghost who cried, "Hamlet, revenge!" It contained, no doubt, numerous elements that have become familiar to us from Shakespeare's drama. Although there have been ingenious attempts to reconstruct the main features of the lost play, the fact remains that it has not survived, and except for a few details the nature of the play remains uncertain.

The transition from the Continental treatments to the English play was first of all a transformation of reported story to enacted story. The narrator yielded the stage to the characters themselves, who now performed the events. Of course, the distinction between a teller and an actor is often one only of degree. An oral raconteur frequently alternates between reporting the events and acting them out, and Saxo's and Belleforest's accounts of the Hamlet story contain scenes in dialogue or monologue that could be acted. Conversely, events in *Hamlet* that are not enacted on stage are reported verbally by one character or another, who functions for the while as a narrator. But for the most part the playwrights have translated the narrator's report into the characters' enactment. There is now no third person, no omniscient observer, no objective voice. The play has no commentator whose statements are the absolute truth of the story; instead, there are the playgoers' interpretations of what they see and hear, and their interpretations of the characters' interpretations of what the latter perceive. We move from an objective narrative world to a subjective dramatic world, a world of appearance rather than of simple fact. In giving up the narrator, the audience loses its privileged certainty and joins the characters in a world of uncertainty and limited knowledge. The playgoers are invited to participate in the same game as that which the characters are playing, which is to discover the objective truth about one another and about themselves.

In its transformation to Renaissance drama the medieval legend has been freely rehandled. Some elements have been dropped, of course, but more features have been admitted to the play, making it a work of considerable length and variety. And the playwright's virtual attack on traditional oral form exemplifies a heavy treatment of the Hamlet story. I attempt here a sketch of the principal kinds of change introduced into the literary tradition of Hamlet by Shakespeare and his immediate predecessor, whose respective contributions I shall not, however, venture to distinguish. I have in mind particularly innovations of plot or form, although I also take notice of the novel inclusion of Danish local color, which is extensive in *Hamlet*.[7]

Time

The narrative versions of the story adhere to the usual practice of oral narrators in presenting the story chronologically from start to finish. Saxo and Belleforest slowly build up to the initial villainy and gradually relax after the revenge.[8] This is the clearest way to proceed, but it is not the most exciting. Shakespeare starts his play with the prospect of war and the mysterious and frightening visitation of a ghost and ends it with a stage piled with corpses.

The drama begins in medias res, after the death of King Hamlet and on the eve of Claudius's marriage and coronation. The important anterior events are given to Horatio and to the ghost to narrate. In 1.1 Horatio describes the pact and the duel of King Hamlet of Denmark and King Fortinbras of Norway, which has led to the current activities of young Fortinbras. In 1.4 the ghost tells how King Hamlet died. It gives both the public account, that a serpent bit him as he napped in his garden, and its own account, that his brother Claudius poured poison in his ear. Since King Hamlet's realm is the entire kingdom of Denmark rather than a portion of it, there is no superior king—no Rørik—to appoint him to office, to receive spoils, or to give a daughter away in marriage; and the government is a monarchy from the start rather than a diarchy. It is simply given (scene 2) that Hamlet and Gertrude were king and queen of Denmark and that the younger Hamlet is their son. The story reaches back no further than this.

Just as the play begins late, so also it ends early, before the story is finished. The corresponding plot in Saxo and Belleforest concludes with Amleth's speech to the Jutes in which he explains and justifies his actions and requests that they acclaim him king, which they do. In the drama the events that shall subsequently take place are implied or promised, since they cannot be narrated. Hamlet, as he lies dying (5.2), bids Horatio—the only survivor who has some understanding of what has happened—tell his story. And just before the arrival of Fortinbras on the scene, Hamlet prophesies

Table of Characters

Present Translation	*Saxo*	*Belleforest*	*Shakespeare*
Rørik	Roricus	Rorique	———
Gervendil	Gerwendillus	Gervvendille	———
Ørvendil	Horwendillus	Horvvendille	Hamlet (elder)
Fengi	Fengo, -onis	Fengon	Claudius
Koller	Collerus	Collere	Fortinbras (elder)
Geruth	Gerutha	Geruthe	Gertrude
Amleth	Amlethus	Amleth	Hamlet
friend of Fengi	(unnamed)	(unnamed)	Polonius
fosterbrother	(unnamed)	(unnamed)	Horatio
fostersister	(unnamed)	(unnamed)	Ophelia
two housecarls	(unnamed)	(unnamed)	Rosencrantz & Guildenstern
king of Britain	Rex Britanniae	Roy des Anglois	England
king's daughter	(unnamed)	(unnamed)	———
Herminthrud	Herminthruda*	Hermetrude	———
Viglek	Wiglecus**	Vviglere	Fortinbras

*Herminthruda: thus emended in Olrik & Ræder; in earlier editions the name is spelled Hermuthruda.

**Wiglecus: thus emended in Olrik & Ræder; in earlier editions the name is spelled Vigletus.

that the election will light on Fortinbras, who has Hamlet's dying voice. When the play ends we confidently assume that these two events will follow in short order. Horatio will give a public account of Hamlet's actions on behalf of Hamlet, who cannot himself do so, and Fortinbras will be successful in his bid for the throne of Denmark.

Between the beginning and the ending one recognizes most of the events of Saxo's and Belleforest's story. The late king's brother weds his widow and assumes the throne. His nephew decides to play the fool. There follow the first test (Ophelia), the second test (Gertrude), and the third test (England). The hero returns to Denmark in humble estate, whereupon he unexpectedly appears at a funeral, his own in the narrative versions, Ophelia's in the drama. Lastly, after some drinking and an exchange of swords (for his own sword has been rendered useless), he slays his uncle. Shakespeare reserves for dramatic enactment the period of time that stretches from the first appearance of the protagonist in the story to the scene in which he accomplishes his revenge.

The playwright then compresses this central slice of the tale in two ways. First, the dramatic time is made to be of considerably shorter duration than it is in the narrative source. Since neither the narrators nor the playwright shows an interest in marking the exact passage of time, it is not possible to calculate just how much time passes in the narrative versions or in the play, but the former do imply the passage of a number of years, while the latter can be imagined to take place within the span of several weeks. The absence of temporal markers has the effect in both of making the events appear to take place in more rapid succession than they logically can. Time seems to march briskly by with unbroken continuity, whereas strictly there is great discontinuity, since the narrator or playwright presents us with only a few select days of the years or weeks of the story. The missing time is not really accounted for, but it exists more logically than dramatically.

The compression of Amleth's years into Hamlet's weeks was an easy matter to accomplish, not only because time is handled vaguely in the narratives but also because the events of Amleth's career seem to take place in quick succession and in a brief period of time. Even Amleth's year-long stay in England, which Shakespeare omits anyway, does not really destroy this impression. The one place in Saxo's narrative where some years must pass is the span of time separating the birth of Amleth and the murder of his father, when the hero is old enough to appreciate what has happened and to develop a sophisticated strategy to deal with his plight. Little time *appears* to pass here, since the narrator immediately follows his mention of Amleth's birth with the account of the uncle's envy and villainy. One must pause and ponder in order to notice that, calculated strictly, the uncle must wait, not days, but years to kill his brother. Shakespeare avoids the whole problem by modifying this part of the story and relegating it to a period before the play begins.

The other form of compression he exercises on the central portion of the tale is the selective enactment of events. There are two major excisions of material found in Belleforest. The first is the hero's plan of revenge, together with virtually all the features that are connected with it in the narrative source. Hamlet does not whittle crooks. Nor, as he departs for England, does he bid his mother clothe the hall with tapestry one year hence and celebrate his funeral. Of all this, Shakespeare retains only the funeral, but it is no part of Hamlet's plan. Hamlet has in fact no revenge plan at all, since the strategy his prototype devised is dropped, and Shakespeare does not substitute another, though he suggests perhaps that in the end Hamlet entrusts himself to divine providence. The other major omission is Amleth's adventure in England. Hamlet is indeed sent there, but is captured en route by pirates, who kindly return him to Denmark, so that the polluted feast, the foreign bride, and the gold-filled sticks disappear from the story. Though the rest of the episode is retained, the playwright compresses and deemphasizes it by having Hamlet merely report it.

The reasons for dropping the original revenge plan and the adventure in England are not difficult to guess. The revenge could scarcely be enacted on an Elizabethan stage, and, more importantly, it would have been an incongruous act for the type of protagonist that Shakespeare fashions and for the age in which the playwright imagines the events to be taking place. As for the foreign adventures of the hero, if retained, they would take much time to dramatize, while they would add very little to the development of the plot. Moreover, there would be the problem of harmonizing the hero's extraordinary abilities in that episode with the more modest abilities he shows elsewhere in the tale. From Belleforest's account of the polluted feast, Shakespeare borrows the hints of the hero's melancholy, supernatural sources of knowledge, and possible abuses by the devil, all representing Belleforest's attempt to explain Amleth's powers in the episode (Commentary, sec.6), and develops them elsewhere in the drama, but he drops the episode itself.

While the playwright compresses the old story, he also expands it with new material, such as the visitations of the ghost, the domestic life of the young woman (Ophelia) and the eavesdropper (Polonius), the traveling troupe of players and their performance, the king at prayer, and the gravediggers.

Character

The primacy of action is a general characteristic of oral narrative and therefore also of literary treatments that reproduce the oral form of a story. Character development and subtle delineation of character are usually foreign. In the fewest of adjectives one can ordinarily sum up the essential traits of the characters, who are defined mostly by what they do, not by what they say or think. In the light treatments of Saxo and Belleforest, little effort is made to elevate character from this position of secondary importance. When a character in Saxo's account appears to be complex, the explanation must be sought, not in subtle characterization introduced by the Danish historian, but in the uneven quality of the telling or in the nature of episodic composition. Of course, a subjective element is not wholly absent from the narrative versions of the story. Saxo and Belleforest elaborate their tale with moral or philosophic observations, some of which they voice in their own person as narrators, while others are given to the characters to state. Moreover, the narrators occasionally reveal the thoughts or emotions of the characters. But in *Hamlet* these features now dominate. They are expressed in the speeches of the characters, especially those of the protagonist, who regularly ponders the philosophic or moral implications of alternative courses of action. The vehicle par excellence here is, of course, the soliloquy, the dramatic convention by which a character may directly communicate his or her private thoughts to the audience.

The reversal of the relative importance and interest of action and character can be illustrated by Shakespeare's introduction of a host of foils to Hamlet. Outside the castle there is Fortinbras, who, like Hamlet, lost his father as well as the succession to the throne. But the aggressive Norwegian prince raises an army to regain the lands lost by his father, and when he is prevented from doing that, he charges off with his army to Poland to gamble his life in fighting over a worthless patch of ground. As Hamlet soliloquizes:

> Rightly to be great
> Is not to stir without great argument,

> But greatly to find quarrel in a straw
> When honor's at the stake. How stand I then,
> That have a father kill'd, a mother stain'd,
> Excitements of my reason and my blood,
> And let all sleep. . . .[9]
> [4.4.53–59]

Closer to home is Laertes, another hot-tempered youth who loses a father. The parallels of their loss and desire for revenge do not escape Hamlet's notice (5.2. 77–78), but the parallels end there. At the death of Polonius, Laertes rushes back to Elsinore in his eagerness for revenge, storms the castle at the head of a mob which clamors to make him king, and angrily confronts Claudius. Hamlet, though he is greatly beloved of the common people (4.7. 16–24), never exploits their numbers.

Then there are Hamlet and Ophelia. After the death of his father and his disappointment in his mother, Hamlet decides to counterfeit madness, but following the breakdown of her relationship with Hamlet and the death of her own father, Ophelia really roams madly through the castle. He contemplates suicide; she is drowned, as Gertrude reports, or drowns herself, as several others believe. In addition Hamlet contemplates the player (2.2) whose passionate recitation of the imagined grief of an imagined person exceeds Hamlet's capacity to express his own passion, which is founded upon reality. And with his rapid and drastic fluctuations of mood, Hamlet admires the stability and balance of his friend Horatio and praises his stoicism (3.2.52–72).

So Fortinbras is prepared to fight, however slight the cause; Laertes craves immediate revenge; Ophelia goes mad; the player and Horatio show great passion or stability; and Hamlet does none of these things, or, rather, he does each one in small measure. It is as though his mind has been analysed into its component parts, which are then personified, intensified, and set free to haunt him and taunt him.

A comparison of the narrative hero with the dramatic hero in respect to the delay in the accomplishment of the revenge illustrates a second way in which Shakespeare has shifted the emphasis from action to character. No Hamlet, it should be noticed, attempts revenge immediately upon his learning of the murder of his father: all Hamlets delay. In Saxo and Belleforest, however, the obstacles to the hero's revenge are completely external in nature. A youth is pitted against a powerful and villainous king and the men who surround him. His task is to accomplish his revenge without losing his own life in the process. To do so he must destroy his uncle and his uncle's allies at a blow, and then justify his actions to the people. Accordingly, he devises a plan and patiently waits until external circumstances permit its execution.

Shakespeare modifies the external obstacles and also adds internal obstacles. Objectively, the killing of Claudius should not be a difficult thing to accomplish, for the king has no reason to expect an avenger and so is not at first on his guard, though by the time that Hamlet has confirmed to himself that his uncle is indeed guilty, the king is fearful of him. But Hamlet does face several obstacles that can be called external. His source of information concerning his uncle's guilt—the ghost—is inherently suspect, and he prefers to confirm the ghost's account independently. Moreover, whereas Saxo's Amleth operates under the pagan code of honor according to which private revenge is the expected thing to do, Shakespeare's Hamlet lives in a Christian world in which both civil and religious law forbid private revenge, though the older code is not without some force, as it is not today. Finally, there is the problem of public justification of the revenge, for the murder is secret, and Hamlet alone is privy to the ghost's version of what happened. If the prince should kill his uncle without convicting him publicly, he might never clear his own name and honor. All these considerations, of which Amleth is free, burden Hamlet. And then there is the subjective obstacle, though it is perhaps not possible really to distinguish cleanly between external and internal obstacles. Hamlet chides himself again and again for his inaction, and the ghost returns to do so also. After all, Hamlet promised the spirit on their initial encounter that he would sweep to his revenge. Throughout most of the play he struggles with the problems of action and inaction, passion and lack of passion. He analyzes these themes almost obsessively, and then wonders whether he analyzes too much, at the expense of doing something. He does not understand his own vacillation, the reason for which is indeed not obvious.[10]

Plot

In Saxo and Belleforest the identity of the regicide is known to all, since the man publicly acknowledges his deed. What he does not confess is his true motive. In the play, however, the killing is done in secret, and the killer does not acknowledge his act, or rather he acknowledges it only in his private prayers. Shakespeare thus complicates the story. Most of the other major new complications in the main plot are logically connected to and to some extent follow from the secrecy of the initial murder.

It is necessary for Hamlet to learn of the murder, or at least to suspect foul play, in order to be motivated to act. The mechanism introduced into the story to accomplish this is the ghost, who, claiming to be the spirit of the murdered man, tells Hamlet how he was killed. But the fact that his source is a ghost creates a new difficulty: how can Hamlet know whether this informant from beyond the grave is trustworthy? Neither Hamlet nor the playgoers can be sure that the spirit speaks the objective truth, since neither witnessed the king's death. In fact, though the audience later hears Claudius acknowledge the murder in his prayers (3.3), Hamlet himself never does hear a confession. The uncertainty concerning the ghost's account rests not simply upon a healthy skepticism but upon the very nature of the spirit. For a Protestant a ghost may be an angel from heaven or a devil from hell (so 1.4. 39–44). If the spirit is a devil in the form of Hamlet's father, it has presumably come to induce him to commit a mortal sin, which would damn him. The ghost itself, however, implies that it is come from purgatory, a category that Hamlet's Protestantism does not acknowledge. The question of the nature of the ghost is never objectively settled in the play.

The uncertainty of the ghost's report leads in turn to Hamlet's desire for independent verification. He confirms the ghost's story to his own satisfaction when he eventually observes the king's response to *The Mousetrap*. But Claudius's negative response can be understood otherwise than as a pang of guilt, for it may be that he interprets the play as representing his mad nephew's regicidal intentions. Indeed, this is how the other courtly playgoers seem to understand the event. The complications caused by the secrecy of the murder do not end here, for though Hamlet manages to satisfy himself and Horatio that Claudius is a murderer, he has not convicted the king in anyone else's eyes. If Hamlet should now kill Claudius, how would he justify the act to others? That it is important to him to be thought something other than a mad regicide is shown by his dying request to Horatio to tell his story to the unknowing.

Yet another byproduct of the murder's being clandestine is that it makes Hamlet's decision to put on an "antic disposition," to play the fool, unclearly motivated, as critics have often observed. So far as Claudius knows, no one but he himself is privy to the truth of his brother's death, so that he has at first no reason to see in Hamlet a potential avenger. Therefore the prince need not adopt the guise of a simpleton or madman to guard his life, as Saxo's and Belleforest's Amleth does. Shakespeare complicates this feature further by making ambiguous the extent of Hamlet's mental stability. At times he is obviously counterfeiting madness. He is then in complete control of himself and, like Saxo's Amleth, enjoys confuting his opponents with double entendres, as in 2.2. But there are other times when he seems hysterical and out of control, as in 1.5, after he sees his father's spirit. In such scenes it appears that events have truly unsettled the mind of the young student. At first Claudius does not so much doubt the prince's distemper as hope to discover its cause so that he may remedy it. Polonius is convinced that the cause is frustrated love; Gertrude thinks it is his father's death and her own overhasty marriage; Rosencrantz and Guildenstern suspect it is frustrated ambition; and Hamlet is not above feeding their individual hypotheses. On the other hand, Hamlet does not know whether he has a murder to avenge or not, so while his uncle is testing him, he tests his uncle. To the antagonist's worry, which is found in the narrative versions of the story, Shakespeare adds an enigma for the protagonist, making the situation symmetrical. *The Mousetrap* simultaneously confirms the suspicions of them both: the king is convinced that Hamlet may try to kill him, and Hamlet is convinced that Claudius killed his father. At this crisis the king makes his move while the prince lets pass his own opportunity to act. When the problem of objective knowledge is solved, Hamlet has still to face the problem of subjective knowledge.

The main plot of the play, which centers, of course, on the Danish royal family, is enriched by two subplots, each concerning the fortunes of a lesser or more remote family. The two families are fashioned from characters that Shakespeare has inherited in most cases through Belleforest's version—minor characters who play cameo roles—or in some cases simply invented. In the episodic composition of Saxo and Belleforest these minor characters tend suddenly to appear on demand and just as suddenly to disappear when the narrator has nothing further for them to do. Appearing only in relation to the protagonist or the antagonist, they have no independent lives of their own in the story. Consequently they possess little or no history when they enter the story and enjoy as little follow-up once they have performed their rather limited function. In the *Vita Amlethi* the hero's foster siblings appear only in the first test; not a word is said about them elsewhere in the legend. While their foster sibling relationship to Amleth explains their loyalty to him, it is a fact without further depth in the story. Similarly, the unnamed eavesdropper participates only in the second test, during which he comes into and goes out of existence. Of him and his history we know only that he is one of Fengi's friends. In the third test there appear the two henchmen of the king who escort Amleth overseas. They are not mentioned earlier, and like the spy they perish within their episode. In his retelling, Belleforest manipulates details but retains the oral form. Thus he transforms the foster sibling relationships, making the amorous foster sister into a young woman who has loved Amleth from childhood and the loyal foster brother into a gentlemen who was reared with the hero, but they are still confined to their single episode. In both Saxo and Belleforest the use of the minor characters is characteristically episodic, and their familial relationships are unemphatic or nonexistent.

Shakespeare extends the story-life (if one may so term it) of these characters by introducing them earlier in the tale and, unless they perish in their inherited episode, reintroducing them later on. Thus we are well acquainted with Polonius long before he plays his old role of eavesdropper, and Ophelia now reappears after the inherited scene in which she is used to test Hamlet. Similarly, Horatio and Rosencrantz and Guildenstern enjoy longer and less episodic story-lives than their prototypes.[11] In addition the playwright gives some of them familial relationships, thereby creating the Polonius family and the Norwegian royal family. The Polonius family is built up from the eavesdropper and the amorous woman (that is, the foster sister as refashioned by Belleforest), to which a new character is added. The most immediate effect of this arrangement is that each event that touches upon Polonius or Ophelia or Laertes gains in magnitude, since it also affects the other members of the family. Ophelia's romance with Hamlet, such as it is, is a worry to her brother and her father. And when Polonius is killed, his death gravely affects both his children; Ophelia's reaction further enrages Laertes; both their responses affect Hamlet. The significance and the impact of an event are made to reach beyond the immediate context in which it occurs. And the immediate context itself is often less spare, since the limit of two active characters to a narrative scene is easily exceeded on the stage.

The three members of the Polonius family balance the three members of the Claudius family, and their fortunes interlock throughout the play, mostly in parallel or contrastive ways.[12] For example, both families are present in 1.2 when Laertes petitions the king to be allowed to return to Paris, whence he came for the coronation, and Hamlet asks leave to return to Wittenberg, whence he came for the funeral; the king grants Laertes' request but denies Hamlet's. In the same scene Claudius censures Hamlet for his continued mourning of his father, and in the the following scene Polonius lectures Laertes on proper behavior in general. Laertes' farewell to his father in 1.3 is followed by Hamlet's encounter with his father's spirit in 1.4–5. Next Polonius sends his servant to Paris to investigate Laertes' behavior (1.6), and presently Claudius and Gertrude bid Rosencrantz and Guildenstern investigate Hamlet's behavior (1.7). Laertes' trip to Paris is followed later by Hamlet's voyage to England, and their returns coincide. Laertes angrily returns to Denmark and bursts into the palace at the head of a mob of Danes (4.5); shortly afterwards Hamlet is returned by pirates to Denmark and sends a somewhat impudent letter to Claudius in which he begs leave to see him (4.6–7). Laertes and Hamlet finally meet again when they grapple with each other during the funeral of Ophelia (5.1), whom they both loved, and once more in the last scene (5.2) when they kill each other in a duel.

The Norwegian royal family of three is composed of the late King Fortinbras, his brother Norway, and the former's son young Fortinbras, who parallel the late King Hamlet, his brother Claudius, and the former's son, young Hamlet. King Hamlet slew King Fortinbras in a duel, after which the succession passed to the king's brother rather than to his son, just as in Denmark when King Hamlet was murdered, his brother somehow popped in between the election and young Hamlet's hopes. But young Fortinbras's eagerness for action is very different from young Hamlet's.

King Fortinbras derives of course from King Collere (Saxo's Koller), for whom Shakespeare invents a brother and successor, simply called Norway in the play. No one has noticed, however, that the prototype of young Fortinbras in Vviglere (Saxo's Viglek), Amleth's adversary in the conclusion of the biography.[13] Belleforest tells how Rorique's son and successor Vviglere harasses Geruthe, complaining that it is the right of the national monarch to appoint the ruler of Jutland; but Amleth appeases him with gifts. In the *Vita Amlethi* Saxo's Amleth now attacks Viglek, taking him by surprise and overcoming him, but Belleforest excises this preliminary battle and skips to the next one, which Amleth's opponent initiates. In other words, the French reteller transfers to Vviglere the aggression that in the Danish telling belongs to Amleth.[14] Vviglere, deciding that he wants all the Danish lands under his rule, declares war on Amleth. The defender dies in the battle, and Vviglere assumes his throne.

Now, the narrative versions of the Hamlet story, like the play, have multiple plots, but in the former they are arranged serially, one after the other, reflecting the oral storyteller's dislike of synchrony.[15] Amleth's three principal adversaries – Fengon, Roy des Anglois, and Vviglere – appear in succession. Shakespeare transposes the third tale to an earlier position, making it occur simultaneously with the first story with which it is then interwoven. He intends to kill off his hero at the end of the play, and the third tale is, of course, the tale of Amleth's death. The aggressive Collere, who has no son, and the newly aggressive Vviglere, who has no father once Rorique's role is dropped from the play, are grouped together as father and son.

A comparison will illustrate the transformation. Belleforest's Vviglere and Shakespeare's Fortinbras are each the son of a king. Vviglere's father gives Jutland to Horvvendille and Fengon; Fortinbras's father loses his lands to King Hamlet. Each youth wants to recover his father's land. Each is pacified for a time. Each initiates a war for land in which he is successful. Vviglere slays Amleth in battle; Fortinbras, returning from battle, arrives in Denmark at the very moment that Hamlet lies dying. Vviglere assumes Amleth's throne; Fortinbras receives Hamlet's dying voice. In short, the story of Prince Fortinbras is essentially the story of Vviglere. The playwright's most remarkable modification here is the division of the battle between Vviglere and Amleth into two more or less simultaneous struggles, one at home and one abroad. Fortinbras's battle in Poland, now deprived of its point, has no real purpose, and Shakespeare boldly develops it into a grandly senseless battle over a worthless piece of ground. Meanwhile, Hamlet is slain in Denmark by another man, but at precisely the advantageous moment Fortinbras shows up at the Danish court, surveys the carnage, which reminds him of a battlefield, treats Hamlet like a fallen soldier, and claims the reward of Hamlet's death, the Danish throne, just as though he, Fortinbras, had been the victor there. The original battle has been analysed into two different battles, but the consequences are the same.

Local Color

Hamlet is set not in the ancient, heroic Denmark of Saxo's story or in the exotically heathen Denmark of Belleforest's version, but in a vague Denmark of the more recent past, a Christian kingdom belonging to the Renaissance world of courts and courtly life and intrigue. Outside the castle are Danes who, like an unseen chorus, respond to the events of the court. Beyond them is a Norway preparing for war, first against Denmark and then against Poland; a tributary England; and a Paris and a Wittenberg where young Danes might go. The hero's uncle is now the king of Denmark rather than merely the ruler of Jutland, and the royal residence is located in Elsinore (that is, Helsingør) at the northeastern tip of Zealand, where in reality the contemporary Danish monarch, whose principal residence was in Copenhagen, had a little fortified palace.

Saxo made no attempt, of course, to introduce local color into the *Vita Amlethi*; what is present is there simply because it is a Danish story told by a Dane. More to the point, perhaps, he made little effort to distinguish Britain and Scotland and their inhabitants from Denmark and Danes in culture, language, or any other way, except to report the name of the Scots queen which, being non-Scandinavian, presumably had a foreign ring to it. But as the name itself is not even Scots, it can hardly be deemed an instance of authentic local color.

Although Belleforest was not a Dane and so might wish to add some genuine Danish touches for the enjoyment of his French public, we find little attempt in his retelling to make Denmark seem Danish or England English or Scotland Scottish. Indeed, Belleforest is not even sure exactly where his tale is set. He wrongly says early on that Jutland is the same as that which is commonly called Ditmarsh, situated on the Cimbric Chersonese. Later the people acclaim Amleth king of Jutland and Chersonese, which, Belleforest incorrectly explains, is today the country of Denmark; however, in the marginal note we are told that Amleth was made king of only a part of Denmark.[16] And though it is true that Belleforest does mention the reputation of Northern countries for sorcery in pre-Christian times and for excessive drinking in general, he does so only to try to explain why Amleth is possessed of extraordinary powers in the episode of the polluted feast and why the participants at Amleth's funeral drink so much.[17]

On the whole, Belleforest has subtracted more Danish elements than he has added. He does not understand much of Old Scandinavia or much of the Scandinavia of his own day. Faced with ambiguous Latin terms and desirous of telling a story that will be intelligible to French readers, he modernizes or familiarizes many details from his sources. The old royal estate becomes a palace with courtiers and pages; Amleth the king's son becomes Amleth the prince; the king's tent becomes a room. More significantly, Belleforest does not understand or appreciate the pagan ideal of revenge, the significance of drinking at funerals, and the ancient institutions of fostering and of sworn brotherhood. As a result he provides Amleth's regicide with a Christian justification, dwells on the excessive drinking habits of Northern peoples, transforms Amleth's foster siblings into a gentleman who had been reared with Amleth and a childhood friend who loved him, and calls the English king barbarous for honoring his oath to his sworn brother. In so doing, Belleforest was being neither unintelligent nor perverse: his aim was to make accessible to a popular readership Saxo's *Vita Amlethi* and its tale set in a now vanished culture, and he no doubt succeeded in doing so.

But if much of the older Danish flavor came in time and with some reason to be misunderstood or dropped from the literary tradition of Hamlet, it came also to be replaced to a large extent by a contemporary Danish flavor. We find the beginnings of it in Belleforest, but it is in Shakespeare's play that for the first time a considerable effort has been made to create an authentic contemporary Danish atmosphere.[18]

Whereas Saxo laid the action of the story primarily in Jutland, and Belleforest in Denmark more generally, Shakespeare moved it to Elsinore, which to Elizabethans was probably the most familiar of any Danish place-name.[19] For one thing there was an impressive new castle there. In 1574 Frederik II had begun the erection of a fortress at Elsinore, and when it was completed in 1585, only some fifteen years before Shakespeare's play was written, it was the finest Renaissance castle in the North. Named Kronborg (that is, Crown Fortress) it was heavily armed and located on the sea overlooking Øresund (the Sound), not, despite Horatio's fear (1.4. 69–71), on the summit of a cliff. But Shakespeare's Elsinore only partially reflects Zealand's Elsinore. The castle is nowhere referred to by name, and there is no mention of a town at the spot. What really made Elsinore known to seafaring nations was not Kronborg itself but its function, which was to force passing ships to pay the hated customs dues imposed on them by the Danish crown. The king got a good part of his revenue from this toll, which was exacted from the many ships that passed through the Sound to or from ports in the Baltic. Since every ship had to stop at Elsinore to pay the Sound dues, the town and its castle were familiar if unwelcome sights to many a seafarer, and Elsinore had many foreign residents and visitors, including an English colony.

An unwitting application of Baltic color possibly appears in Polonius's instruction to Reynaldo (2.1.7): "Inquire me first what Danskers are in Paris." Since *dansker* is Danish for "Dane," commentators on *Hamlet* commonly believe that Polonius employs a good Danish word here, and gloss it as such, but in Shakespeare's time the Danish word *dansker* in the sense of "Dane" had not yet been formed.[20] The word then in use was *dansk*, which meant "Dane" or "Danish"; and *dansker* was actually an adjective meaning "of or from Danzig." In English usage of the time *Danske* ordinarily meant "Danzig" or "of or from Danzig"—or, rarely, "Danish" or even "Denmark"!—and *Dansker* referred to a "person of or from Danzig," that is, a Danziger. Then a free city under the protection of the Polish king, Danzig (Polish *Gdańsk*) was one of the important ports in the Baltic for English ships. What then did Shakespeare have in mind when he wrote "Danskers"? Did the confusing similarity of the terms for Denmark, Danzig, and their inhabitants mislead him into believing that *Danskers* properly meant "Danes"? Or did this confusing terminology together with the perhaps unclear political status of Danzig make it appear to him that Danzig was part of the Danish realm, in which case Shakespeare's Danskers are rightly the natives of Danzig but wrongly imagined to be Danish politically? Or could it be that the playwright was not at all mistaken and merely represents Polonius (that is, the Pole) inquiring about fellow ethnic Poles abroad?

However that may be, Shakespeare's references to Wittenberg are an accurate use of Danish local color. Hamlet, Horatio, and perhaps Rosencrantz and Guildenstern are represented as being students at the university there. Englishmen did not seek out the University of Wittenberg, Luther's unversity, but Danish nobles and scholars of the late sixteenth century entered at the rate of over four a year.[21]

Although some of the personal names in the play betray an acquaintance with things Danish, the majority of them are ultimately Greek (Laertes, Ophelia), Latin or Neo-Latin (Claudius, Cornelius, Marcellus, Polonius), or Italian (Horatio, Barnardo). Shakespeare simply gives most of the characters foreign names, just as in Saxo's tale the Scots queen bears a non-Scandinavian name. But the playwright does employ a few Danish names. Voltemar (Q1), Valtemand (Q2), Voltemand (F1), and so forth (1.2.34) are obviously corruptions of the Danish name *Valdemar*. Yaughan (5.1.60) probably represents *Johan*, and Yorick (5.1.184) may derive from *Georg,* the Danish form of *George*.[22] Gertrude was certainly inspired by Belleforest's Geruthe, but as a woman's name it was known to both England and (in the form *Gertrud*) Denmark. I have already mentioned that *Hamlet* was an English name, though its choice was obviously determined by the similar Danish name in Saxo and Belleforest.

The two most interesting Danish names in *Hamlet* are those of Rosencrantz and Guildenstern, variously given in different editions of the play as Rossencraft (Q1), Rosencraus and Rosencrans (Q2), Rosincrane (F1); and Gilderstone (Q1), Guyldensterne (Q2), Guildensterne (F1). Obviously, Danish names, especially long names, caused some difficulty to the English ear. Unlike the names mentioned earlier, which are all common given names, that is, ordinary names that an Englishman would hear and use in informal association with Danes, the names *Rosenkrantz* and *Gyldenstjerne* are family names and quite aristocratic.[23] Indeed, the families are two of the most noble and prominent in Danish history. Each name derives from the family's coat of arms, *Rosenkrantz* (that is, "rose wreath") from the garland of red and white roses on a helmet, and *Gyldenstjerne* ("golden star") from a seven-pointed star on a blue field. Several Rosenkrantzes and

Gyldenstjernes were likely to be present, along with members of other influential families, at any important state occasion or ceremony. At the coronation of Christian IV in 1596 10 percent of the approximately 160 noblemen in the procession were either a Rosenkrantz or a Gyldenstjerne, and of the 20 councillors who placed the crown on the new king's head 2 were Gyldenstjernes.[24]

Members of these families being in such abundant supply, one should perhaps resist the temptation to identify a particular Rosenkrantz and particular Gyldenstjerne whose names Shakespeare found it apt to adopt and associate together in his drama. In the *Hamlet* literature many such identifications have been offered in apparent ignorance of the profusion of actual Rosenkrantzes and Gyldenstjernes. Any historical Rosenkrantz whom a scholar comes across is likely to be seized upon and suggested as the source of the name in the play. But if Shakespeare knew Rosenkrantz and Gyldenstjerne as the names of two particular contemporary Danes and not simply as the names of two noble families, and if temptation be yielded to here, the best candidates seem to be Frederik Rosenkrantz (1569–1602) and Knud Gyldenstjerne (1575–1627), whose full names were Frederik Holgersen Rosenkrantz of Rosenvold and Stjerneholm, and Knud Henriksen Gyldenstjerne of Aagaard. They were friends as well as kinsmen, each studied at Wittenberg, both men returned together to Denmark in 1591 and in 1592 both went together to England for about a year. If Shakespeare had any real persons in mind when he borrowed these names, it was probably these two, whose lives ran somewhat parallel to those of their namesakes.[25]

I content myself with one final example of Shakespeare's use of contemporary Denmark, namely, the drinking habits of the Danes.[26] The king's personal physician, writing in mid-sixteenth-century Denmark, observed:

> Most Danes, particularly the nobility, are inordinately given to drink and could spend both day and night emptying goblets. They especially find it impossible to hold a wedding, banquet, or party without the one's urging the other to keep drinking, while doing the same himself, until they (if you will excuse my

> saying) spew out the ale again, and in the presence of the servers and guests take care of another matter under the table without the slightest shame. And when one of them, half or wholly unconscious, must be brought to bed, the fact causes immense jubilation and is the occasion for roars of laughter.[27]

Frederik II of Denmark was a lover of drink, and it was no secret that his death in 1588 was caused by excessive drinking. Nor was his son Christian IV a moderate drinker. This Danish intemperance seems to have been well known to the English. Fynes Moryson observed that "the Danes passe (if it be possible) their neighbour Saxons in the excesse of their drinking." John Stow claims that "it would make a man sick to heare of their drunken healths."[28] And in *Pierce Penilesse* Thomas Nashe wrote:

> The Danes are bursten-bellied sots, that are to bee confuted with nothing but Tankards or quart pots, and *Ovid* might as well haue read his verses to the *Getes* that vnderstood him not, as a man talk reason to them that haue no eares but their mouths, nor sense but of that which they swallowe downe their throates.[29]

Shakespeare's Danes are also heavy drinkers. When Hamlet first encounters Horatio, he says:

> But what is your affair in Elsinore?
> We'll teach you to drink deep ere you depart.
> [1.2.174–75]

And the prince acknowledges the Danish reputation for drunkenness:

> This heavy-handed revel east and west
> Makes us traduc'd and tax'd of other nations.
> They clip us drunkards.
> [1.4.17–19]

Shakespeare also knew of a special drinking custom beloved of Danish kings, the firing of cannon to accompany each skole, or toast.[30] In 1603 when the Danish king had a banquet prepared for him on an English ship off Kronborg, an Englishman recalled that each health was followed by 6, 8, or 10 cannon shots, for a total of

160 shots while the king was on board. At another banquet in 1606 each skole uttered by a member of the royal party was straightway followed by the sound of drum and trumpet and the firing of cannon.[31] Shakespeare's Claudius observes the same custom when he promises:

No jocund health that Denmark drinks to-day,
But the great cannon to the clouds shall tell,
And the King's rouse the heaven shall bruit again,
Respeaking earthly thunder.
[1.2.125–28]

And that evening the king drinks toasts to a chorus of kettledrum, trumpet, and shots (1.4.7–16). This royal practice is referred to once more in the final act when Claudius says

Give me the cups,
And let the kettle to the trumpet speak
The trumpet to the cannoneer without,
The cannons to the heavens, the heaven to earth,
"Now the King drinks to Hamlet."
[5.2.274–78]

Shakespeare's use of so many contemporary Danish features implies that, for whatever reason, he made a real effort to create an authentic, if not consistent, Danish atmosphere. In this respect he far surpasses not only the meager efforts made by Saxo and Belleforest but also those found in other Elizabethan works of fiction concerning Danes or Denmark, in which there is not much local color and what there is of it is not skillfully employed.[32] Shakespeare differed from his contemporaries in both the quantity and the quality of his use of actual foreign elements. In the case of *Hamlet* we should also remember that Denmark was a politically more powerful nation then than now and that it was particularly topical in England around the time that *Hamlet* was written. A year after the death of Frederik II of Denmark in 1588, his daughter Anna married James VI of Scotland, who in 1603 succeeded Elizabeth on the English throne as James I.[33]

But perhaps as important a reason as any for the playwright's many Danish touches is that he himself had easy access to information about Danes and Denmark. In the late sixteenth century there were English actors, musicians, and composers in the service of the Danish court.[34] In 1579 a company of English entertainers was received by Frederik II at the port town of Crempe, where the king had a residence, and with some changes in personnel it remained in the employ of the Danish court until 1586. It was probably this group that gave a public performance in the town hall courtyard in Elsinore in 1585, for the king often held court at his newly completed castle, and as a rule the entertainers followed the court.[35] Most pertinent are several other English entertainers who entered the service of the court in 1586, only a year after the completion of Kronborg. According to the royal accounts, William Kempe and a boy were employed for two months beginning June 17, for which they received thirty-six daler. At the same time a troupe of five entertainers was engaged, including George Bryan and Thomas Pope. They stayed from June 17 to September 18. These three men – William Kempe, George Bryan, and Thomas Pope – are all well-known later colleagues of Shakespeare. All were members, together with Shakespeare, of the Chamberlain's Men as reorganized in 1594, and all are listed among the principal actors in the First Folio. So Shakespeare had access to firsthand information touching upon Denmark in general and Elsinore and the royal court in particular from his own coworkers in the theatre.

The Shakespearean use of contemporary Danish features did not always have the effect that the playwright presumably sought. In 1721 a Danish tourist in London was enticed into Drury Lane by a notice of "Hamlet Prince of Denmark." The disconcerted playgoer noted in his diary that it was "a good tragedy taken from Saxo Grammaticus, but mixed with inventions in connection with the names of places and persons that are not suitable to the story itself. Among other things there are introduced Rosenkrantzes and Gyldenstjernes, whose families are certainly very old but doubtless a thousand years younger than the story of Hamlet."[36] He did not jot down Shakespeare's name, which was just beginning to be known in Denmark around 1700. The first complete Danish translation of *Hamlet* was made in 1777,[37] and *Hamlet* was first performed on the Danish stage in 1813.

Shakespeare's own countrymen were also affected by his borrowings from a more recent Denmark. From the end of the eighteenth century many foreigners, especially Englishmen and Germans, began making the pilgrimage to Elsinore to visit the site associated with the Danish prince.[38] What they found there was a Kronborg which had been restored after having been all but destroyed by fire in 1629; in 1658–60, moreover, the Swedes had occupied the castle and done much damage to it. Tourists also found an extensive garden or park, in which there were, inter alia, a little summer palace named Marienlyst and an English garden. The latter, which had been completed in the last decade of the eighteenth century, was an allegorical garden in accordance with the Romantic taste of the times. It was divided into a portion representing the Earthly Realm with its delights, and a portion standing for the Kingdom of Heaven. One wandered from the Earthly Realm to the World's End. There was a little creek there, on the earthly side of which a Hermit's Hut stood, representing loneliness and solitude, and on the far side a grave mound with a broken column. From there one climbed up to the Kingdom of Heaven, the hope beyond the grave.

Some tourists were inevitably disappointed to discover in Elsinore a castle that was too recent for Hamlet's time, but others cheerfully began to remake Elsinore to fit their expectations. English tourists renamed the King's Garden as Hamlet's Garden, for by at least 1805 there appear English engravings with the title "Hamlet's Garden" under pictures of Marienlyst. Presently the empty allegorical grave in the garden came to be called "Hamlet's Grave," probably not because the visitors at first thought that Hamlet actually lay buried there but because it was natural to assume that a grave in Hamlet's Garden was intended to represent Hamlet's grave, that is, a memorial grave in honor of the Shakespearean hero.

Towards the middle of the nineteenth century, however, the notion of an allegorical or memorial marker was forgotten, and tourists began to take the grave to be the actual burial place of the historical Hamlet. It must be understood that Danes and those few foreigners who knew from Saxo that Hamlet lay buried in Jutland evidently had nothing to do with furthering these traditions, which seem to have been a kind of tourist lore devised and transmitted primarily by Englishmen, who were unfamiliar with the history of the Hamlet story. But once it came about that some persons interpreted the spot literally, others inevitably denounced it as a deliberate fraud, which it really was not.

Unfortunately, all that changed in 1857 when a Dane named Nathanson, who had leased Marienlyst to set up a bathing establishment, decided to exploit the confusion. He sought and received permission from the Marienlyst Committee of the Elsinore City Council "to arrange 'Hamlet's Grave' in a manner corresponding to the legend."[39] Whatever legend he may have had in mind, it is obvious that he was less a restorer than a businessman, for what he did was to move the broken column away from the grave mound and install it in a walled enclosure behind Marienlyst, where he could charge visitors thirty-two skilling to visit the marker. At the same time he got permission to improve the situation of what was then known as Marie Spring (Marie Kilde) but by 1859 was being called Ophelia Spring (Ophelia Kilde).

Fortunately, Nathanson's commercially motivated fraud has had its day, and there is no longer a grave of Hamlet at Elsinore to move, puzzle, or outrage the tourist. The present-day visitor to Elsinore will find merely a pleasant city and an interesting castle and the old gardens, which are separated from the castle by a section of the town.[40] And he or she will probably be a little moved and a little disappointed, the former because it is after all Elsinore, the latter because Hamlet's association with Elsinore is an Elizabethan playwright's invention and because the town and its fortress can scarcely match a pilgrim's fantasy.

Life
of
Hamlet

1. The Beginning

Rørik put Ørvendil and Fengi in charge of the defense of Jutland. They succeeded their father Gervendil, who had been jarl of the Jutes. When Ørvendil had ruled for three years and won outstanding glory as a viking, King Koller of Norway, who rivaled him in great deeds and fame, thought it would add to his own reputation if he could overcome the viking in arms and dim the luster that surrounded him. He sailed around scouting the sea until he came upon his ships. There was an island in the middle of the sea at which the vikings put in, each on his own side. The two chieftains found the shores pleasant and inviting, and the outward beauty of the place made them want to explore the spring-fresh interior of the woods, wander in its meadows, and roam through the remote places of the forest. It was there that Koller and Ørvendil chanced to meet without any of their men.

Ørvendil was the first to speak: "How do you wish to fight? I myself prefer the way that requires the fewest men. For winning the award of courage, a duel will be the best form of combat, since it will rely only on our own bravery and exclude the help of other men."

Koller admired the young man's brave talk, and said: "Since you have left it to me to choose how we should fight, I think it is best when only two men fight, free of the tumult of others. It is more direct and more quickly decided. We are agreed about this and hold the same opinion.

"But since the outcome is in doubt, we should treat each other reasonably and not be so carried away by our feelings that we forget what is owed the dead. Our minds are full of hatred for each other, but in the end respect should replace harshness. Even though our intentions separate us, the laws of nature bind us together, for we are united by them however much hatred keeps our minds apart. Out of respect for each other let us set this condition, that the victor shall hold a funeral for the loser. Everyone agrees that this is the final act of good will, and no man of honor refuses to do it. Let both of our armies forget their anger and perform this duty together. Our anger should cease after death; our feud should stop at the grave. Although there is hatred between us while we both live, we should not be so cruel as to persecute the other's dead body. The winner will enhance his reputation if he holds a magnificent funeral for the loser. For the man who shows honor and respect to the enemy he has killed wins for himself the favor of the survivors. He conquers the living with his kindness when he treats a dead man courteously.

"There is another kind of misfortune, no less grievous than death: a man may lose a limb and yet live. I think we should concern ourselves as much for this state as for death, for it often happens that fighting men survive but are crippled. Most men consider this fate worse than any other because death takes a man's memory away, but a living man can never forget the crippling of his own body. We should alleviate this misery also. Let us agree that if one of us cripples the other, he shall pay him ten marks of gold. If a man ought to sympathize with others in their misfortunes, should he not have all the more pity on his own? No one can ignore his own welfare. If he does, he is his own slayer."

They both agreed to these conditions, and began to fight. Neither the strange circumstances of their meeting nor the springtime pleasantness of the spot could prevent them from deciding things by the sword. Such fury came upon Ørvendil that he was more eager to strike his enemy than to guard his own body. Throwing aside his shield, he grasped his sword with both hands. His boldness was rewarded. He struck Koller's shield again and again, hacking it to pieces, and finally hewed off one of his feet so that he fell lifeless to the ground. To keep their bargain he gave him a king's burial with a large and magnificent barrow and held a huge funeral feast. Then he pursued and killed Koller's sister Sæla, who was an experienced viking and a skillful fighter.

After three years of courageous battling, Ørvendil gave Rørik the best of the spoils and the pick of the plunder in order to win higher favor with him. Relying on their friendship, he asked for and obtained in marriage Rørik's sister Geruth, who bore him a son Amleth.

2. Fengi's Villainy

Fengi burned with envy at his brother's great success, and decided to do away with him. A good and honorable man dare not feel safe even among his own kinsmen. When an opportunity came to murder him, with bloody hands he sated the lust to kill that was in his heart. Then he added incest to fratricide by taking the wife of the brother he had butchered. For a man who gives in to one crime rushes headlong into a second, since one goads him to the next. He was bold and shrewd in covering up the horrible thing he had done. He justified his crime by pretending that he had acted from good will and disguised the murder as an act of duty. For although Geruth, he said, was so gentle that she would not hurt anyone, even slightly, she had been the victim of Ørvendil's stormy hatred, and it was to protect her that he had slain his brother, since he thought that a woman who was so mild and gentle should not have to put up with her husband's overbearing arrogance. The motive he alleged was accepted, for lies are believed by powerful men in whose halls buffoons are sometimes held in favor and accusers are honored. Without delay Fengi shamelessly embraced his wife with arms that had murdered, following up one outrageous crime with another.

3. Amleth's Counteraction

Amleth saw this and feared that he might make his uncle suspicious if he behaved intelligently. So he feigned madness and pretended that his mind had been damaged. With this cunning he not only concealed his cleverness but also guarded his life. Every day he sat on the ground at his mother's hearth, unkempt and listless, and tossed dirt upon himself. With his soiled face and his skin smeared with putrid slime, he looked like a grotesque madman. Whenever he spoke, he spoke like a fool, and whatever he did he did with utter foolishness. Why should I say more? You would not have called him a man at all, but an absurd monster due to a derangement of fate.

While sitting at the hearth and sweeping the ashes with his hands, he sometimes made wooden crooks which he hardened in the fire. Their ends he fashioned into opposing hooks so that they would cling tightly if fastened to something. When he was asked what he was doing, he answered that he was making sharp spears to avenge his father. His reply caused no little jeering because everyone thought his efforts were pointless and ridiculous. But this very project helped him afterwards in carrying out his plan.

4. The First Test

It was his dexterity which gave the more thoughtful observers their first suspicion of his cunning. For skill in a trifling craft indicated hidden ability in the craftsman: they could not believe that he was dull of mind when he was so skillful and artful in the use of his hands. Finally, he always watched over his pile of fire-hardened sticks very carefully. Some men therefore said that his mind was active enough and that he was only playing the simpleton in order to conceal his intelligence, all the time hiding some deep purpose under a cover of foolishness. They thought that the best way to expose his cunning was to bring him together with a beautiful woman in some secluded place where she could tempt him with the pleasures of love; for by their very nature emotions turn into passion so quickly that they cannot be skillfully concealed, the impulse being too powerful to be checked by cleverness; if, then, he was only pretending to be witless, he would immediately give in to pleasure when the occasion was offered. And so men were assigned to lead the young man horseback riding into a distant part of the forest to test him.

Among them there happened to be a certain foster brother of Amleth. He was mindful that they had been brought up together, and he valued his memory of their early life together more than his present orders. He went along with the other escorts to warn rather than to trap Amleth, not doubting that it would be Amleth's death if he should reveal even a small sign of sound mind, and above all if he should have sexual relations before their eyes. That was also plain enough to Amleth himself. For when they bade him mount his horse, he purposely did so backwards so that he faced its tail, and then he began to bridle the tail as though he intended to guide the galloping horse by that part of it. With this ingenuity he frustrated his uncle's plan and foiled his trap. The sight was ridiculous enough—the horse galloping away without reins while its rider guided it by its tail.

Amleth went on and encountered a wolf in a thicket. When his companions said that he had come across a rather young horse, he replied, "In Fengi's stable there are too few of this kind fighting," thereby gently but wittily cursing his uncle's wealth. They said that he had given a clever answer, and he declared that he had meant to do so, since he did not want people to think that he ever indulged in lying. Amleth desired to be held an honest man, but he mixed truth and cleverness in such a way that you could not call his words false, although they did not betray their real meaning.

As he was passing along a beach and came upon the rudder of a wrecked ship, his companions said that he had found a huge knife. "Yes," he said, "it is suitable for cutting a huge ham"—by which he really meant the sea, since its vastness matched the size of the rudder.

They also came by some sand dunes and told him to look at the flour, meaning the sand. He replied that it had been ground fine and bleached by the storms of the sea. His companions praised his retort, and he said that he had put it rather well.

Now they purposely left him alone so that he might feel freer to act upon his passion. The woman whom his uncle had dispatched met him as though by chance in a dark spot, and he would have had sexual relations with her if his foster brother had not secretly warned him of the trap. He had been considering how he might aptly and secretly warn the young man in order to forestall his dangerous urge. Taking a gadfly that was flying past, he placed under its back a piece of chaff that he had found on the ground, and drove it toward the place where he knew Amleth to be. By this act he did the incautious youth a great favor. The message was interpreted just as ingeniously as it had been sent, for when Amleth saw the gadfly together with the straw which it wore embedded in its back, he examined it very carefully and perceived that it was a secret warning to watch out for treachery. Frightened and suspecting a trap, he took the woman in his arms and brought her to a distant and nearly inaccessible bog where he could more safely do what he wished. After they lay together he earnestly begged her not to tell anyone of it, and she promised her silence as readily as he asked for it. They had had the same foster parents in infancy, and the fellowship of their early rearing made the girl feel a strong friendship for Amleth.

After he had been escorted back home, everyone jokingly asked whether he had indulged in love-making, and he acknowledged that he had ravished the girl. Asked next where he had done it and what he had used for a cushion, he said that he had lain upon an animal's hoof, a cock's comb, and some roof beams. To avoid lying he had gathered pieces of all these things when, tempted by the girl, he was setting out. The bystanders greeted this account with much laughter, although in his joking he had told the truth. The girl was also questioned about the matter, and she claimed that he had done no such thing. They believed her denial all the more willingly when they found that the housecarls did not know what had happened.

Then he who had marked the gadfly to send the warning, wishing to show Amleth that it was to his ingenuity that Amleth owed his safety, said that recently he had been singularly devoted to him. Amleth's replay was quite apt. Not wanting him to think he was indifferent to the value of the warning, Amleth answered that he had in fact noticed something suddenly flit by with a stalk of chaff clinging to its rear end. His answer roused the others to laughter, but Amleth's friend was pleased by its cleverness.

5. The Second Test

Everyone was worsted and unable to open the hidden lock of the young man's cleverness. But a certain one of Fengi's friends, who had more confidence than he had judgment, said that no ordinary trap would expose Amleth's intricate cunning; he was too obstinate to be reached by trivial efforts, and so it was useless to pit a simple test against his complex cunning. Thinking the matter through, he said, he had his upon a subtler way, one which would not be hard to put into effect and would without a doubt lead them to learn what they wanted to know. Fengi was to pretend some important business and purposely make a show of departure. Amleth was to be enclosed alone with his mother in her bedroom, but before that it should be arranged for a man to station himself, unknown to the two of them, in a dark part of the room to overhear carefully what they should talk about; for if her son was at all sane, he would not hesitate to speak out to his own mother and would not be afraid to confide in the very woman who gave him birth. He himself eagerly volunteered to play the spy to show that he was just as ready to carry out a plan as to devise it. Pleased by the idea, Fengi made a pretense of a long journey and departed.

The man who had proposed the plan went secretly to the room in which Amleth was being enclosed with his mother and concealed himself under the straw. But Amleth had a remedy for the trap. Fearing that someone might secretly eavesdrop, he resorted at first to his usual silliness, crowing like a noisy rooster and beating his arms together as though he were flapping wings. Getting up on the straw, he began to leap all around to find out whether anything lay lurking there. When he perceived a lump beneath his feet, he clove the spot with his sword, stabbing the man who lay underneath, dragged him out of his hiding place, and slew him. He cut up the body, cooked the pieces in boiling water, and dumped them through the hole of the outhouse for the swine to eat, strewing the putrid refuse with the wretch's limbs.

Having in this way foiled the plot, he went back to the room. When his mother cried out and began to weep for the folly of her son to his face, he said: "Shameless woman, why do you try to conceal your immense crime with false tears? You revel like a whore in this abominable marriage of yours, incestuously embracing your husband's murderer and filthily caressing and fawning upon the man who slew the father of your son. So do mares couple with those who have overcome their mates. That is how animals behave, pairing with one after another. By your actions you show that you have wholly forgotten your former husband.

"As for me, I do not play the fool for nothing, because I do not doubt that the man who murdered his own brother would rage just as viciously against his other kin. It is better for me to play the fool than to reveal my intentions, and by acting the complete simpleton to guard my life. But in my mind the eagerness to avenge my father remains, and I am waiting for the right setting and the fitting time. There is a place for each thing. Against a dark and harsh mind one must use guile. But it is a waste of time to cry for my madness when you should be lamenting your own disgrace. Weep not for the flaw in another's mind, but for that in your own. As for the rest, keep this all to yourself." With these reproaches he wounded his mother and brought her back to leading a life of honor, showing her that her former passion was better than her current delights.

Fengi returned, and though he searched for a long time, he could not find his spy anywhere. Everyone said he had not seen him at all. When Amleth was jokingly asked whether he had come upon any trace of him, he reported that the man had gone to the outhouse and fallen through the hole; overwhelmed by all the filth, he was devoured by the swine that go around there. Although he acknowledged the truth, his answer struck those who heard it as funny since it seemed to be senseless.

6. The Third Test

Fengi now strongly suspected his stepson of deception and wished to do away with him, but he did not dare do so for fear of angering Amleth's grandfather Rørik as well as his own wife. He decided to have the king of Britain kill him so that he himself could pretend to be innocent, another man doing the deed. In his desire to conceal his own cruelty, he chose to soil a friend rather than to bring dishonor upon himself.

As Amleth was departing, he secretly told his mother that when a year had passed, she should deck the hall with woven hangings and celebrate his funeral as though he were dead. He promised that at the time he would return.

Two of Fengi's housecarls set out with him. With them they carried a letter carved on wood (for that was once a common kind of writing material), bidding the king of Britain put to death the young man who was sent to him. But while the two were sleeping, Amleth searched their coffer and found the letter. He read its contents, scraped off what had been carved, and substituted different runes, changing the sense of the message and transferring his own doom to his companions. Not content with shifting his own death sentence onto others, he added an entreaty, falsely using Fengi's name, that the king of Britain give his daughter in marriage to the very intelligent youth he was sending him.

When they reached Britain, the messengers went to the king and handed him the letter which they believed was the instrument of another's destruction, but really contained their own sentence of death. The king said nothing about it, and welcomed them all courteously and hospitably. But Amleth scorned the entire banquet of the king as though it were an ordinary meal. To everyone's surprise he turned away from the plenteous feast, touching the drink no more than the food. All were astonished that a foreign youth should look with disdain upon the splendid delights and extravagant dishes of the royal table as though they were some peasant's fare. When the feast was over and the king was bidding his friends good night, he had one of them sneak into his guests' bedroom so that he might secretly listen to what they talked about during the night.

When his two companions asked Amleth why he had treated yesterday's feast as though it had been poison, he said that the bread was polluted with blood, the drink had a tang of iron, and the meat reeked of a human cadaver as if infected with the smell of death. He added that the king had the eyes of a thrall and in three ways the queen behaved like a thrallwoman. In short, he found fault with his hosts even more than with the meal. Then his companions began to taunt him with his old defect of mind, mocking and deriding him because he blamed what he should have praised and found fault with good things and because he vulgarly attacked an illustrious king and a lady of polished manners, showering extremely improper reproaches upon praiseworthy persons. When the king heard all this from his housecarl, he declared that a person who made such observations had either more than mortal wisdom or more than mortal folly, since he revealed in so few words either the heights or the depths of mind.

Then the king summoned his overseer and asked him where he had gotten the bread. When the man said that the king's own baker had baked it, the king asked where the crop had grown from which the flour was ground and whether there was a sign of anyone's having been killed there. The man answered that not far away from where they were, there was a field full of old bones of slain men which still showed clear traces of ancient slaughter. He said that he had sown the field with grain in the spring, supposing it to be more fertile than the other fields and hoping for the best possible yield; so the bread might perhaps have picked up a bad taste from the gore. When the king heard this, he surmised that Amleth had spoken the truth. He also wanted to know where the pork came from. The overseer said that because of negligence their own swine had wandered out of their sty and fed on the rotten corpse of a thief, so that a flavor of decay might have entered their flesh. After the king found that Amleth's judgment in this matter was also true, he asked what liquid the drink had been brewed with. Learning that it had been brewed of honeycombs and water, he had the spring shown him and had the men dig deeply at the site. He found several rusty swords and concluded that from their tang the water had gotten its off-taste. Others relate that he found fault with the mead because in drinking it he perceived that some bees had fed upon the paunch of a corpse and imparted the bad flavor to their honeycombs, so that it reappeared in the taste.

The king saw that Amleth had correctly explained the causes of the flavors he had censured. Since he recognized that the ignoble eyes which Amleth charged him with having had to do with a stain on his birth, he went secretly to his mother and asked who his father really was. She denied submitting to any man except the king. When he threatened to get the truth out of her by torture and forced her to confess, he learned that he had been fathered by a thrall.

While he was ashamed of his low birth, he was pleased with the young man's perceptiveness and asked him why he had reproached the queen for behaving like a thrallwoman. But though he resented the fact that his guest in an evening conversation called his wife's courtliness into question, he soon had to hear that she was actually born of a thrallwoman. Amleth said he had observed in her three faults showing the habits of a thrall: first, like a thrallwoman she had covered her head with her mantle; second, she tucked up her gown for walking; third, after picking her teeth with a toothpick, she chewed the bits of food she had picked out. Finally, in order that he might see that his wife was a thrall by birth as well as by habit, Amleth told him that her mother had been captured in war and made a thrallwoman.

The king worshiped his intelligence as if it were something more than mortal. He gave him his daughter in marriage and embraced whatever he said as a witness from the heavens. As for Amleth's companions, he had them hanged on the following day in order to comply with his friend's wish. But Amleth acted as though this favor were an injury and pretended to be angry, so that the king gave him as compensation an amount of gold, which Amleth later melted down secretly and poured into some hollow sticks.

After spending a year with the king, he obtained leave to depart and returned to his own country, taking none of his regal treasures with him except for the sticks filled with gold. When he reached Jutland, he dropped his current role in favor of his former one, purposely switching from respectable behavior to foolishness.

Covered with filth, he walked into the hall where his funeral was being held. Everyone was aghast, since a false rumor had spread word of his death. But horror finally gave way to laughter as the celebrants jokingly taunted one another for the fact that the person whose funeral they were celebrating, thinking he was dead, was both alive and present. When they asked him about his companions, he showed them the sticks he was carrying and said, "Here they are, both of them." It is hard to say whether there was more truth or wit in that remark, for though most of them thought he answered senselessly, he kept to his habit of telling the truth, holding forth the wergild as though it were the slain men themselves.

7. Amleth's Revenge

Wishing to increase the celebrants' merriment, Amleth joined the servers and worked at plying the drink. So that his loose clothing should not hamper his walking about, he girded on his sword. But since he kept drawing the sword and purposely cutting his fingers with its point, some of the bystanders had an iron nail struck through his sword and sheath. To smooth the way for his plot, he plied the nobles with drink after drink until he had gotten them so drunk that they could not stand up and went to sleep where they were, making the hall their bedroom.

Amleth saw that they were in a fit state for his trap and judged that the time to carry out his plan had come. In a fold of his clothing he put the sticks he had once fashioned and then went back into the room in which the nobles lay strewn all over the floor, sleeping and vomiting in their drunkenness. He cut away the supports of the hangings his mother had made, which covered the inside walls of the hall, so that they fell to the ground. He placed them upon the sleeping men, and with his crooks he bound them together so skillfully and tightly that none of the men who lay beneath was able to rise, however powerfully he tried. After this he set fire to the building. The flames grew and spread until they covered the entire hall, consuming it and burning to death all the men inside, whether they were deep in sleep or trying in vain to get up.

From the hall he went to Fengi's bedroom (his housecarls had earlier escorted him to his tent), where he took the sword that hung by Fengi's bed and replaced it with his own. Then he awakened his uncle and informed him that his nobles were perishing by fire, and that Amleth was there, armed with his old crooks and eager to exact the revenge he was owed for the killing of his father. On hearing this, Fengi leapt out of bed but was cut down while in the absence of his own sword he was trying in vain to draw another's.

A brave man and deserving to be remembered forever! He shrewdly played the fool and with an amazing pretense of folly kept hidden an intelligence more sublime than mortal. By his cunning he not only saved his own life but also managed to avenge his father. Because of his skillful defense of himself and his vigorous vengeance of his father, it is hard to say which was the greater, his courage or his cleverness.

8. The Aftermath

After slaying his stepfather, Amleth was afraid to bring his act before the people, of whose verdict he was unsure. Until he could learn which way the common folk were tending, he judged it best to stay out of sight. In the morning the people living nearby, having seen the fire during the night and wanting now to find out what had brought it about, saw that the hall had fallen to the ground in ashes, but in searching through its ruins, which were still warm, they found only the shapeless remains of bodies burnt in the fire. The flames had so utterly consumed everything that not a single clue remained from which they might learn the cause of the disaster. They did, however, see the body of Fengi, pierced by a sword, his clothes drenched with blood. While some of them expressed anger and some sorrow, others were secretly delighted. The former grieved for the death of their leader; the latter rejoiced that the murderer's reign had come to an end. So the onlookers responded with divided opinion to the killing of their king.

The calmness of the common people gave Amleth the courage to come out from hiding. He sent for those men who he knew clung to the memory of his father, and went to the meeting place where he addressed them in this way: "Nobles, if the wretched death of Ørvendil caused any of you grief, do not grieve at the sight of the misfortune before you now. Do not grieve, I say, those of you who have remained loyal to your king and faithful to your father. The corpse you see is not that of a king but of a fratricide. The sight was far more sorrowful that time when you saw with your own eyes your king, miserably slaughtered by this—I won't say brother—criminal murderer. With your own tear-filled eyes you saw Ørvendil's mangled limbs, his body covered with gashes. Who can doubt that this fierce butcher robbed him of his life so that he might then strip our land of its freedom? The hand that slew him made you thralls. Is there a man so mad that he would prefer Fengi's viciousness to Ørvendil's righteousness? Recall how kindly, justly and mildly Ørvendil cared for you. You remember how you lost a gentle king, a just father, how you got in his place a tyrant, an assassin, how he took away your rights, contaminated everything, polluted the land with crime, hung a yoke on your necks, snatched away your freedom.

"But all that is now past. As you can see, the man who was responsible for it has been overwhelmed by his own crimes. The murderer has paid for his misdeeds. What man of ordinary sense, seeing this, could take this favor as an injury? What man in his right mind could be sorry that the crime has recoiled upon the criminal? What man would cry over the murder of a blood-stained executioner or the just killing of a cruel tyrant?

"The person responsible for what you see is here. I acknowledge that it was I who avenged my father and my country. I performed the duty that fell on all of us alike. What you should have done along with me, I did alone. I had no partner in this fine feat, no ally to help me. I know that you would have joined me if I had asked you, since you doubtless have remained loyal to your king and fond of your prince, but I wished to take vengeance on these criminals without risk to you, thinking that I should not burden other shoulders when I believed my own were strong enough.

"These men I have already burned to ashes, but Fengi's trunk I have saved for you yourselves to cast into the fire so that at least on it you can slake your thirst for just revenge. Come, gather around quickly, heap up a pyre, burn the impious body, cook the abominable limbs, scatter the guilty ashes, strew the savage embers. No pot or barrow should hold what is left of his cursed bones. No trace of the murderer should remain. There should be no place for his contaminated limbs in our land. No region should contract an infection from them. His execrable corpse must not pollute the sea or soil. I myself have done the rest, and left this one job for you. These are the proper rites for a self-made king; this is the fitting funeral for an unnatural murderer. The ashes of the man who stripped his country of freedom should not be covered by his country's soil.

"Why should I go over my own troubles, reveal my own suffering, review my sorrow?—you know it all better than I do. Marked for death by my stepfather, despised by my mother, and scorned by my friends, I passed the years in misery, spent my days in sorrow, and lived an uncertain life full of danger and fear. In short, my entire life has been one of suffering and tremendous adversity. Among yourselves you often sighed in secret for my folly: 'There is no one to avenge his father,' you said, 'no one to pay out the killer.' For me this was a secret sign of your affection, and I saw that you still remembered the killing of your king. Is any man so hardhearted and rigid that he is not softened by compassion for my grief or moved by my troubles? Have compassion for your foster son, grieve for my misfortunes, you, whose hands are clean of Ørvendil's blood. Pity also my poor mother and be glad that the shame of the woman who was once your queen has been removed. With her woman's body she had to bear the burden of a double disgrace each time she embraced the brother and killer of her husband.

"To keep my desire for revenge hidden I concealed my understanding and pretended to be witless. You may now see for yourselves whether it succeeded and reached its goal. I am content for you to decide the matter. But now it is your turn—trample the murderer's embers under your feet! Scorn the ashes of the man who defiled and debauched the wife of the brother he butchered, who struck his lord, betrayed his king, brought in harsh tyranny, took away your freedom, heaped incest upon murder.

"Accept me in a noble spirit as the agent of a just punishment and the warrior of rightful revenge. Grant me the honor I have earned, and support me by looking upon me kindly. I have wiped the stain off our country, rid my mother of her shame, driven out the tyrant, slain the killer, and escaped my uncle's plotting by counterplot. If the man were still alive, his outrages would grow daily. I grieved for the wrong done to my father and fatherland. I rid you of the man who carried his fierce rule beyond what men should do. I ask you to acknowledge my service, honor my intelligence, and, if I have earned it, grant me the kingdom. You have in me one who has done you a great service, no degenerate heir to his father's power nor a murderer, but the lawful successor and the dutiful avenger of the murder of a kinsman. You have me to thank for winning back your freedom, for driving out the tyrant's reign, for lifting the oppressor's yoke, for striking down the murderer's rule, for trampling the despot's scepter under foot. I have freed you of your thralldom and led you to freedom, given your honor and your glory back to you, got rid of the tyrant, conquered the butcher. My reward is in your hands. You know what I have earned. From your generosity I ask my wages."

The young man's speech moved everyone, some to compassion, others even to tears. When their grieving had settled down, they enthusiastically and unanimously acclaimed him king. For they all put great hope in his intelligence, since with his deep cunning he had devised so great a deed and seen it through with almost unbelievable enterprise. Many of them marveled that he had managed to conceal so ingenious a plan for so long a time.

9. The King of Britain

After doing all this in Denmark, Amleth had three ships lavishly fitted out, and returned to Britain to see his wife and father-in-law. As his personal guard he took on young men of proven ability, richly clothed and armed. For he wished to look magnificent in every way, just as he recently had been lowly in appearance, and whereas he once worked at playing the pauper, he now indulged in luxury. He had a shield made for himself on which he had a man paint fine pictures of all his deeds, beginning with those of his earliest youth. He carried it as a record of his prowess, and with it he increased his fame.

On the shield you could see painted the murdering of Ørvendil, Fengi's fratricide and incest, the evil uncle and the foolish nephew, the crooks, the stepfather's suspecting and the stepson's pretending, the various tests, the woman who was to seduce him, the gaping wolf, the rudder they came upon, the sand they passed, their entry into the forest, the gadfly with the straw, the young man being warned by a sign, the eluded companions, and his secretly having sexual relations with the girl. And you could see the royal hall pictured, the queen's meeting with her son, the killing of the eavesdropper, how he was then cooked, dropped through the hole, tossed to the swine, and how his limbs lay strewn in the filth, left to be devoured by the animals. You could also see how Amleth discovered his companions' secret while they were sleeping, how he scraped off the runes and put others in their place, how he disdained the feast and scorned the drink, how he criticized the king's face and the low behavior of the queen. You could also see pictured the messengers on the gallows, the young man's wedding, his voyage back to Denmark, the celebration of his funeral, his showing them his sticks when they inquired about his companions, his acting as a server, his purposely drawing his sword and cutting his fingers, the sword riveted with a nail, the swelling festivity and noise, the growing gaiety, the hangings placed upon the men when they were asleep, his fastening them together with his crooks and wrapping up the men tightly as they slept, his putting a firebrand to the room and burning up the feasters, the hall consumed by fire and collapsing, his going to Fengi's bedroom, taking Fengi's sword and putting the unusable sword in its place, and how with his own sword the king was slain by his stepson. All these things a skillful craftsman painted upon his battle-shield, reproducing objects and events in pictures with the finest handiwork. Amleth's men bore gilt shields to increase their own splendor.

The king of Britain received them kindly and welcomed them with a lavish and regal banquet. During the feast the king asked eagerly whether Fengi was alive and well, and his son-in-law told him that there was no use in asking after his health since he had perished by the sword. With a flood of questions he asked him who Fengi's slayer was and found out that he who told him of the killng had also done the killing. On hearing this he was secretly shocked because he realized that it now fell on him to avenge Fengi, which he had once promised to do: for he and Fengi had once mutually sworn that one should avenge the other. And so the king was drawn one way by his fondness for his daughter and by his love for his son-in-law, and the other way by his affection for his friend and especially by the bond of his oath as well as by the very sanctity of a mutual vow, which it was impious to break. In the end he set the ties of kinship aside and chose to keep his oath. Putting sacred duty before family bonds, he turned his thoughts to revenge. But since it was unholy to violate the sacred rights of a guest, he decided to have someone else carry out the revenge, hoping that he would appear to be guiltless if the matter were done in secret.

And so he concealed his plot with friendliness and hid his intent to do harm under a show of eager goodwill. Because his wife had recently died of illness, he bade Amleth undertake a mission to arrange a new marriage for him, telling him that he was extremely pleased with his remarkable shrewdness. He declared that there was a woman reigning in Scotland whom he desired very much to marry. But the king knew that she not only wanted to remain a virgin but was a cruel and arrogant woman who hated her suitors and always put her would-be lovers to death, so that every one of those many men had paid for his suit with his life.

Although the mission was dangerous, Amleth did not shrink from the job asked of him, and set out, relying in part on his own attendants and in part on those of the king. When he reached Scotland and was not far from the queen's estate, he went to a meadow by the wayside to refresh the horses. Attracted by the beauty of the spot and lulled into drowsiness by the pleasant rushing of the stream, he thought of napping, and posted some men to keep watch at a distance.

When the queen heard of their arrival, she dispatched ten men to spy on the approaching foreigners and their equipment. One of them, quicker-witted than the rest, slipped past the guards, came boldly and stealthily up to Amleth, and so gently removed the shield on which Amleth had laid his head when he was going to sleep that he did not disturb his slumber, even though he was lying on it, or awaken any of the men in his company. He wanted to bring back to the queen not only a report but also a concrete token. And just as skillfully he stole the letter that Amleth was bringing from the coffer in which he kept it.

When these objects had been brought to the queen, she carefully scanned the shield, and with the help of the words appended to it she made out the gist of the story, realizing that this was the man who with a most subtle and cunning scheme had taken revenge on his uncle for the murder of his father. She also looked at the letter containing the suit for her hand, but she removed what had been written because she hated the thought of marrying an old man and desired rather the embraces of a younger. Then she wrote a different message, making it look as though it had been sent to her by the king of Britain and signed with his name and mark. She pretended that she was being asked to wed its bearer. She also included an account of the deeds that she had learned from Amleth's shield so that his shield would serve to support her letter, while her letter interpreted his shield. Then she told her scouts to put the shield and the letter back in their places again, using the same trick against Amleth as she found he had once fooled his companions with.

Meanwhile, Amleth realized that the shield had been stolen from under his head. He shut his eyes again on purpose and cleverly acted as though he were asleep, hoping that by pretending to be asleep he might get back what he had lost when he really was asleep. For he thought that the thief would probably try to deceive him again, since he had already succeeded once. He was right. As the scout silently came up, wanting to put the shield and the letter back in their old places, Amleth leapt up, grabbed him, and bound him. Then he roused his men and went to the queen's dwelling.

He greeted her on behalf of his father-in-law and handed her the letter with the king's seal. After Herminthrud—that was the queen's name—had taken it and read it, she praised Amleth's deeds and shrewdness, saying that Fengi had gotten the punishment he deserved, and that the unfathomable cleverness of Amleth had devised a plan beyond human judgment, since he had with his inpenetrably deep mind not only avenged his father's death and his mother's adultery but also by notable acts of courage won the kingdom from the man who had so often plotted against him.

"Therefore," she said, "I am surprised that so intelligent a man as you has made one bad slip, that of your marriage. Although your fame is almost more than human, you have stumbled into a low and common match. For your wife's parents are thralls even though good luck graced them with the titles of king and queen. In seeking a spouse, a wise man should not look for beauty but for noble birth. Therefore, if you wish a proper match, you should judge the family and not be won over by looks, for although looks are alluring, their empty ornament has tarnished the honor of many a man. There is, moreover, a woman, as nobly born as you, whom you could take. I myself, whose means are not slight and whose birth is not humble, am a fitting wife for you, since you do not surpass me in royal wealth nor outshine me in the splendor of your forebears. I am a queen and, if I were a man, would be a king; or, what is more to the point, the man I deem worthy of my bed becomes a king, since I give him my kingdom together with myself. My scepter and my hand go together. I am doing you no small favor in offering you myself, since for other men it has been my practice to follow my refusal with the sword." And so she urged him to make over to her his favor and marriage vows, and to see that birth was better than beauty. With these words she fell upon him with a close embrace.

Delighted by the maid's gracious words, Amleth put his arms around her and returned her kisses, saying plainly that the maid's desire was also his. Then a banquet was held, friends and nobles were summoned, and the marriage was celebrated. After that he went back with his bride to Britain, having bidden a strong band of Scots follow closely behind and help in case of any treachery.

Upon his return to Britain he was met by the king's daughter, to whom he was still married. Though she complained that he had slighted her by replacing her with a mistress, she said that it was not right for her to put her hatred of his mistress before her love of her husband, and would not so reject her spouse as to say nothing of the trap that threatened him. For as a pledge of their marriage she had their son, and her feeling for him ought to put her in mind of her love for her husband. "He will hate the mistress who has supplanted his mother," she said, "but I will love her. No crisis will quench my passion for you; no envy will put an end to my love or stop me from revealing to you the evil plot against you and the treachery I have discovered. Beware, then, of your father-in-law, since you yourself have reaped the harvest of your mission and in spite of his wishes boldly seized all the fruit for yourself." With this warning she showed that she loved her husband more than her father.

As she was saying this the king of Britain came up, embraced his son-in-law closely but with little affection, and invited him to a feast, wishing to hide the deceit he intended behind a show of generosity. Aware of the deceit, Amleth did not show fear, but bidding two hundred horsemen follow him and putting on a cuirass under his shirt, he complied with his host. He preferred the danger of accepting the king's false invitation to the shame of declining, so much did he wish to maintain his honor in all things.

Amleth came riding up to the open leaves of the gate, but the king attacked him when he was just under the arch, and would have driven his spear through him if the hard cuirass had not stopped it. Slightly wounded, Amleth went to the place where he had told the young Scots to wait for him. He dispatched to the king his new wife's scout, the man whom he had once captured. The man was to bear witness that he had secretly taken from its coffer the letter intended for his mistress. He was thus to transfer the blame to Herminthrud and with this calculated excuse clear Amleth of a charge of treachery. But the king did not cease from pursuing him vigorously as he fled, and slew most of his troops.

On the following day, though he would be fighting for his life, Amleth completely despaired of his power to make a stand, so that he made his army appear to be larger than it really was. Taking the fallen bodies of his men, he propped some of them up against stakes, leaned some against nearby rocks, and set others on horseback like living men, leaving them all fully armed and arranging them in order of battle as if they were about to fight. There were no fewer men in the wing of the dead than in the band of the living. It was an astonishing sight: dead men dragged out to battle, corpses forced to fight. The plan served him well, for when the sun shone upon them, the bodies of the dead looked like a huge army. The lifeless corpses of the dead restored the troops to their original number so that you would not think that any man had been lost in the slaughter of the previous day. Terrified at the sight, the Britons fled before the fighting began, conquered by the very dead whom they had subdued when they were alive. I do not know whether this victory owed more to cleverness or luck. The king was slow to flee and was slain by the pursuing Danes. Amleth won the battle, and after much plundering and looting in Britain, he returned with his wives to his own land.

10. King Viglek

Meanwhile Rørik had died, and Viglek had become king. Harassing Amleth's mother with every kind of insolent behavior, he had stripped her of her royal wealth, charging that her son, in seizing the kingdom of Jutland, had cheated the king of Lejre, whose right it was to give and take away positions of power. Amleth took this treatment with so much restraint that when he presented Viglek with the best of the spoils from his recent victory, he seemed to be repaying an injury with kindness. But afterwards Amleth seized a chance of avenging himself, attacked him, overcame him, and so went from being a secret to an open enemy. Jarl Fjaller of Skaane he drove into exile, and the story goes that he fled to a place called Undensakre, which is unknown to my countrymen.

After this Viglek collected fresh forces from Skaane and Zealand and sent messengers to challenge Amleth to fight. Amleth, with his remarkable perception, saw that two choices surged around him, one of which was shameful and the other dangerous. He was aware that if he accepted the challenge, he would be putting his life into danger, but if he refused he would dishonor himself as a warrior. As he considered his feats of prowess, his wish to save his honor won out, and his powerful desire for glory weakened his fear of death, since he did not want to bring his name into shame by meekly turning his back to his fate. He saw also that there was as great a difference between a common life and a noble death as there was between scorn and honor. Moreover, he loved Herminthrud so much that he was less concerned about his own death than about her future widowhood, and he carefully considered how he might arrange a second marriage for her before the start of the war. But Herminthrud said that she had the courage of a man and promised that even on the field she would not desert him, saying that any woman who was afraid to join her husband in death was detestable. However uncommon her vow, she did not keep it. For when Amleth had fallen in battle with Viglek in Jutland, she yielded herself to be the victor's spoil and share his bed. All vows of women become void with changes in fortune, are dissolved by the shifting of time, and disappear with the play of fate, for their faith stands on slippery feet. Though they are quick to promise you something, they are slow to keep it. Slaves of pleasure, they leap headfirst and gaping in their continual longing for something new, and forget the old.

This was the end of Amleth. If he had had as much luck as he had cleverness, he would have equaled the gods in fame and surpassed the labors of Hercules in the glory of his accomplishments. There is a field in Jutland that contains his barrow and is named after him. After a long and peaceful reign, Viglek died of illness.

Commentary: The Sense of the Events

1. The Beginning

Rørik appoints Ørvendil and Fengi as successors of their father Gervendil, who was jarl (earl) of Jutland.[1] It is thereby implied that the peninsula of Jutland is part of a unified kingdom of Denmark ruled by Rørik. Most of the exposition that follows is given over to an account of the martial and marital successes of Ørvendil, in the course of which Geruth and Amleth are introduced.

Jarldom or Kingdom?

Since Jutland was governed by Jarl Gervendil, one expects his successors to be jarls as well. Saxo, however, consistently refers to Ørvendil and Fengi (and later Amleth) as kings, and there can be little doubt that they enjoyed royal status in the native Jutish legend. Though Denmark had not always been gathered, as it was in Saxo's day, into a single realm under a single ruler, Saxo promotes Zealand by making the kings at Lejre on Zealand the rulers of Denmark from the earliest times and reducing other rulers in rank.[2] Saxo's apparent demotion of Gervendil from king to jarl has introduced this slight inconsistency into the story. But even as kings, the rulers of Jutland are somehow subordinate to the Zealand monarch, whose right to a portion of the spoils of battle

Ørvendil manifestly acknowledges when he gives Rørik the pick of the plunder, as Amleth later (sec. 10) does Viglek.

Monarchy or Diarchy?

More puzzling than the status of Jutland as a jarldom or kingdom is another obscurity. How do Ørvendil and Fengi hold one office? Do they reign simultaneously or in succession? The latter alternative seems to be supported in Amleth's speech to the Jutes (sec. 8), in which he appears to describe Ørvendil and Fengi as successive rulers. But the speech is more vague than clear on this point, and such an arrangement would be difficult to harmonize with the two brothers' initial appointment as their father's successors, which implies that both men hold office from the first. If, moreover, Fengi were not already king, he would not automatically assume his brother's throne at the latter's death, since in any case the office was not hereditary. Without a doubt, Ørvendil and Fengi share the rule, but how do two kings share a kingdom?

The most likely answer is that the brothers were imagined to have divided the kingdom between themselves such that one took charge of the land and the other of the sea. In this case Ørvendil is of course the sea king, Fengi the land king, and the result of Ørvendil's death is, not that Fengi becomes king for the first time, but that he now has the entire kingdom to himself. Such an allotment is known in old Danish tradition and is mentioned elsewhere in Saxo.[3] In one account (Saxo 7.1.1–3) a certain King Olaf decides before his death to divide his realm between his two sons, Frodi and Harald. One of them is to have the kingdom of the land and the other that of the sea, in yearly shifts. As the first sea king Frodi suffers terrible losses because the men he takes along with him are all recently married and yearn for their wives. When it is Harald's turn he selects only unwed men. He is as glorious as his brother is inglorious, but his success is also his downfall, for the envious Frodi has him killed, just as in our story Fengi murders Ørvendil from envy at his success. Since the legend of Harald and Halfdan, of which this is the beginning, and the legend of Amleth are historically related, the parallel has special force. The notion that Ørvendil and Fengi are diarchs, one a sea king and the other a land king, must somehow lie behind Saxo's account, but Saxo withholds, or does not know, the necessary details.

Ørvendil's Holmgang

After three years as a rover, Ørvendil's martial career is crowned by a splended victory in single combat against the king of Norway, after which he wins the favor of Rørik, weds his daughter, and begets a son. The duel exemplifies in a concrete scene the general statement that King Ørvendil is a glorious viking. By his actions he is shown to be brave (he prefers duels to battles), skillful (he wins), and honorable (he keeps his secret pact with Koller). The portrait of Amleth's father is that of an ideal warrior-king at the height of his career. He gains fame, wealth, and a fine marital alliance. He is or possesses almost everything that the Old North held worthy of being or having.

Features of the formal Scandinavian holmgang ("duel," literally "islet-going") are to some extent recognizable in the encounter of Ørvendil and Koller, though not in their classic heroic form.[4] For here no challenge precedes the fighters' meeting, and an island as the site of the duel is almost a matter of chance. King Koller of Norway seeks out the famed Ørvendil in the hope of overcoming him in arms, and he finds him at sea. Then, it appears, both parties just happen to put in at the same island, on opposite sides, and when the two kings eventually come across each other alone in the middle of the island, their meeting owes more to their love of natural beauty than to Koller's tracking or to an earlier arrangement. Moreover, the practice of ransoming oneself has been misunderstood or perhaps intentionally inverted.[5] For now it is not the loser who may ransom his life (one could usually get by with three marks of silver) but the winner who must compensate him for damages, and with no modest sum—ten marks of gold. Saxo is familiar with the old custom, for he describes it correctly elsewhere (7.2.13). Although the duel episode certainly draws upon elements of the classic holmgang, the tone is as much romantic and chivalric as it is heroic.

2. Fengi's Villainy

The man who most values what Ørvendil has is Fengi, who murders his brother and weds the widowed Geruth. The killing is not hidden, but what Fengi does not publicly acknowledge is his true motive for the slaying. Saxo's narration of Fengi's deeds is rapid and summary, but it is sufficient to show that Fengi is the antithesis of his brother. Ørvendil duels; Fengi murders. Ørvendil honors his private agreement with Koller; Fengi broadcasts a false interpretation of his own crime. Ørvendil wins Geruth by gaining her father's favor; Fengi, by doing away with her husband. Fengi's actions repeat those of his brother, but ignobly.

When Fengi murders his coruler, passing it off as justifiable homicide, he remains in office as sole ruler without any formalities appointive or elective. The diarchy was only a temporary arrangement answering to the fact that the previous ruler left two sons. Without comment, the diarchy becomes a monarchy. Fengi is a usurper in that he deprives his brother of his half of the rule and takes it for himself, but he does not cheat Amleth of a chance at the kingship.

3. Amleth's Counteraction

Amleth's Disguise

The story shifts from Fengi to Ørvendil's son, whom custom designates as the agent of revenge. Amleth is a mere youth, and he is outnumbered, for to be effective he must deal not only with the king but also with the king's supporters. His initial response to his uncle is therefore defensive rather than offensive. By his guise as a fool, made credible by the sudden death and replacement of his father, Amleth means to suggest that he is incapable of exacting vengeance.

Amleth's Crooks

While sitting at the hearth Amleth sometimes fashions wooden crooks that he hardens in the fire and guards carefully. When he is asked about them, he explains that he is making sharp spears to avenge his father with ("acuta se referabat in ultionem patris spicula praeparare"). It is generally held that Amleth is punning here, since Old Icelandic *krókr* 'crook' can also mean "clever trick."[6] If so, in the native version of the tale Amleth replied that he was preparing crooks / tricks for the revenge of his father. But if this was the point in the story that Saxo knew, it obviously has been lost in the retelling, both because the pun cannot be rendered in Latin and because here Amleth is made to reply that he is preparing *spicula* 'spears', not *uncos* 'crooks'. But I doubt whether a pun was ever there. It does not appear in the surviving Icelandic version of the Hamlet story, the *Ambales Saga*, where the hero fashions stakes rather than crooks. Nor is the hypothetical pun superior to the metaphor in Saxo's telling. When Amleth describes his humble crooks as spears, his interrogators interpret his words as foolish, but the metaphor is justified inasmuch as the crooks are actually a part of his arsenal. What Amleth's adversaries cannot foresee is the extremely unconventional means of revenge he is preparing.[7]

4. The First Test

Before Amleth and his companions come upon the girl, and while Amleth presumably continues to ride his steed backwards, they pass in succession a wolf, a rudder, and some sandhills. Each of these provides the occasion for a minor testing of the hero.

The Wolf

When they see a wolf in a thicket and the others say that Amleth has come across a young horse, he retorts, "Perpaucos huiusmodi in Fengonis grege militare," which I render, "In Fengi's stable there are too few of this kind fighting." Since the point of the retort is not obvious and the meaning of some words uncertain, any translation of the line necessarily reflects an interpretation of it. Does, for example, *grex* in the phrase "in Fengonis grege" refer to a herd (of animals) or to a troop (of men)? Apart from the words themselves, the only clue we have to the point of Amleth's retort is Saxo's comment that it is a gentle but witty curse on his uncle's wealth; and Amleth's escorts praise it as clever.

Olrik takes *grex* to refer to Fengi's warriors, but since Amleth's retort is not then congruent with Saxo's explanation of it, Olrik emends *divitias* wealth in Saxo's explanation to *vitia* 'cowardice', making Saxo comment instead that Amleth's retort is a curse on his uncle's cowardice:

> "Of that kind of horse," he replies, "there are certainly not many in Fengi's army!" wherewith – says Saxo – he spoke sarcastically of Fengi's cowardice. His uncle was no chieftain who provided food for wolf and raven by campaigning.[8]

Hermann Schneider, however, sees in the wolf a metaphor for Fengi himself:

> Amleth must have said more or less: "At the court of my wealthy uncle there are many foals, but thus there is only one there; namely a wolf." And this wolf would then of course be Fengi himself. An excellent comparison, since the wolf is the symbol of greed, bloodthirst, and wantoness![9]

While Schneider's interpretation has the virtue of requiring no actual emendation of the Latin text, it has the fault of depending upon an exceedingly free translation that amounts to a rewriting of what Amleth says. Schneider slips in a reference to a "wealthy uncle" who has "many foals," words that are not really Amleth's. At the same time he entirely ignores Amleth's reference to fighting ("militare").

Even so, it is conceivable perhaps that Amleth might say, "In Fengi's court there are very few of this kind" (that is, wolves), while he means that really there is only one of them, his uncle. I say it is conceivable, but it is neither witty nor a curse on the king's wealth, which, if Saxo understands the incident correctly, is the point of the remark.

Hans Sperber believes that the wolf is a metaphor, not for Fengi, but for Amleth! He points out that "wolf" occasionally is used metaphorically for a murdered man's son, who may in the future become dangerous.[10]

> The wolf, then, is Amleth himself, not by virtue of any general likeness, but from the fact that he, and he only, is charged with the duty of avenging his father. Translated into plain language, he says: I am the only one who is thinking of revenge; I wish there were more of us.[11]

But the term "wolf" is never, to my knowledge, employed alone as a metaphor for the son of a slain man; that is, "wolf" is not sufficient of itself to suggest this notion, since the metaphor is not established and familiar. Rather, the son of a murdered man can be called a wolf because, like a wolf, he is potentially fierce and dangerous. A Northern reader or hearer would associate wolves with qualities such as these rather than with the idea of vengeance. Finally, Sperber's rendering, like Schneider's, does not qualify as a curse on Fengi's wealth.

Ideally, Amleth's retort should make sense both when its referent is taken to be "horse" and when it is taken to be "wolf"; otherwise, there is little point in introducing Amleth's comment by having his companions call the wolf a horse. It is simplest to assume that at first Amleth seems to make a remark about horses; that is, from the viewpoint of his companions (and of the reader) the fool appears to accept the proposed identification of the wolf as a young horse. But then they (and we) perceive that his remark could as well have to do with wolves, so that it is unclear which one he intends and whether his words spring from folly or wit. Thus, on the one hand he may mean that in Fengi's stable there are too few *horses* fighting (= campaigning), possibly with the implication that Fengi, unlike Ørvendil, wins no fame in battle. On the other hand he may mean that in Fengi's stable there are too few *wolves* fighting (= laying waste), a wish that wolves may ravage the king's stable of horses.[12] The latter answers well to Saxo's explanation that Amleth is cursing his uncle's wealth. The idea of a curse is admittedly purchased at the expense of understanding *perpaucos* 'very few' here in the sense of *nimis paucos* 'too few', following Saxo's first commentator, Stephanius.[13] Even so, this line of interpretation seems to force the least and explain the most.

The Rudder

When they ride along a beach and see the rudder of a wrecked ship, Amleth's companions tell him that he has found a huge knife, and he agrees, saying that it is suitable for cutting a huge ham ("eo, inquit, praegrandem pernam secari convenit"). Saxo explains that Amleth really means the sea since its size matches that of the rudder. If that is correct, why does Amleth say "ham" when he really means "sea"? The answer must be that he says both. Though a pun on "ham" and "sea" is not possible in Latin, it is in Old Danish, in which the singular *laar* 'thigh' and the plural **laar* 'coastal waters' are homonyms.[14] So Amleth in fact says that the huge knife / rudder is suitable for cutting a huge ham / sea. As in the case of the wolf, Amleth's companions cannot be sure which referent he has in mind.

The Sandhills

When Amleth and his escorts now pass by some sandhills and the latter tell him to look at the flour, he replies that it has been ground fine and bleached by the storm of the sea ("arenarum quoque praeteritis clivis, sabulum perinde ac farra aspicere iussus, eadem albicantis maris procellis permolita esse respondit").[15] Here it is Amleth's companions who initiate the wordplay, if, as it has been thought, they are punning on Old Icelandic *melr* 'sand' and *meldr* 'meal, flour'.[16] But the visual similarity of piles of sand or flour is sufficient to suggest the metaphor, whether a pun was present or not, so that as with *krókr* a play on *melr / meldr* is possible but not necessary. In any case Amleth again bests Fengi's men when he speaks of the stormy sea metaphorically as an immense mill: the flour / sand was milled and bleached by the stormy sea. As before, Amleth's referent is ambiguous.

Evidently this brief and seemingly unimportant incident in Amleth's career was familiar enough to a Northern audience two centuries before Saxo that it could be recognized in allusion. For it is mentioned in a fragment of a poem attributed to an Icelandic or Norwegian skald Snæbjörn:

> Men say that the nine maidens of the island-mill are moving the host-fierce mill of the skerries out beyond the skirts of the earth, they who long ago ground Amloði's meal.[17]

That is, men say that the nine maidens of the island-mill (= the nine daughters of Ægir = the waves of the sea) are moving the host-fierce mill of the skerries (= the sea) out beyond the skirts of the earth, they (= the waves) who long ago ground Amloði's meal (= the sand). Snæbjörn, describing the stormy sea, speaks of it as a mill which grinds down skerries and made the sands long ago. He employs "Amloði's meal" as a kenning for sand in an apparent allusion to such an incident as that which we know only from Saxo's account. Snorri Sturluson, who quotes the strophe in a discussion of poetic synonyms for the sea, comments simply, "Here the sea is called Amloði's mill."[18]

Amleth's Foster Sister

The purpose of the main test is to determine whether Amleth is sexually responsive and therefore sane. The results are again inconclusive. Unfortunately, so much of the episode itself is unclear that we must have an overly abbreviated account of it. Since the girl is Amleth's foster sister and readily allies with him, it is impossible to imagine that she has conspired with Fengi to entrap Amleth or even that she is at all aware of the plot. Yet the trap obviously is arranged in advance, and Saxo explicitly says that she is sent by Fengi. Finally, if Fengi needs only an attractive girl to determine whether Amleth is capable of passion, his choice of the youth's foster sister as lure is as surprising as the choice of his foster brother as spy, since ordinarily the two would be expected to show each other loyalty. As for sexual relations between foster siblings, however such a connection may have been regarded, Saxo the moralist has nothing to say, whether he finds nothing very reprehensible in the encounter or prefers not to detract from the nobility of his hero. One recalls that in the *Ambales Saga* the hero weds the daughter of King Tamerlaus, who is in some sense his foster father.

If one attempts to imagine a fuller version of the episode in which at least some of these details would be plausible, the simplest is perhaps the following. Amleth and the girl are suspected to have an erotic relationship. Fengi dispatches her to a place in the woods, giving her one reason or another but saying nothing of the men whom he sends at the same time to bring Amleth to the spot and to spy on the two. Unaware that they are being watched, they are about to have sexual intercourse when Amleth is secretly warned. Then, playing the madman, he carries the girl off into a fen where no one can observe them.[19]

Amleth's Foster Brother

Saxo's unsatisfactory presentation of the foster brother (*collacteus*) is another sign that the present episode is somehow too abbreviated or poorly told. Why is it that among Fengi's henchmen there is Amleth's own foster brother? Fengi cannot be ignorant of their relationship, for the institution of fostering was common in Old Scandinavia and the matter would be public knowledge. Fengi's including the foster brother in such a delicate position of trust makes sense only if the latter has previously sworn an oath of allegiance to the new king and is in his employ. This is the crucial detail that must be missing from Saxo's telling of the episode.

In this instance, moreover, confirmation is furnished by the Northern analogues to Saxo's story, where we find foster figures who are reminiscent of Amleth's *collacteus*. In the *Ambales Saga* Gamaliel is the friend and wise counselor of King Salman, Ambales' father. After Faustinus's murder of Salman, Gamaliel consents under certain specified conditions to serve Faustinus as his counselor, and so swears the usual oath of loyalty to him. He honors his oath by giving the new monarch good and honest advice, while at the same time he does his utmost to ensure that Ambales and Amba come to no harm. He acts in effect as Ambales' foster father. In the revenge episode Gamaliel does not even leave the hall with the rest of the Christians after they have been warned by Ambales. As a man of honor he observes his promise of loyalty to the heathen king, though he does not go so far as to warn him of what is afoot. For this reason Ambales himself must carry Gamaliel outside and restrain him until everything is quiet, that is, until Gamliel is released from his oath by the death of the king. In Saxo's account of Harald and Halfdan, the boys' father, King Harald, is killed by Frodi. Regin, their foster father, purchases their safety from Frodi by swearing an oath to inform the king of any plot the boys should conceive against him. In the similar Icelandic tale of Hroar and Helgi, Froði kills King Halfdan, father of Hroar and Helgi. Froði forces the folk to swear allegiance to him. Since the boys' foster father Regin has family in Denmark, he has little choice but to swear an oath of allegiance to the new king. In all these tales the loyalty of the foster figure towards the hero or heroes springs from affection or friendship of long standing, and towards the villain, from a sacred oath coupled with a strong sense of personal honor. In short, the man's sympathies are with the protagonist while his allegiance is promised to the antagonist. The Northern analogues show that a foster figure of one kind or another was a traditional feature of this story in its Northern form. Like Gamaliel and Regin, Amleth's foster brother must have sworn an oath of allegiance to the king after the murder of the late king. And like Gamaliel he must be in the king's service. Fengi would inevitably be aware that the two youths were foster brethren, but deemed the relationship to be of little importance once he had received from the one a formal declaration of loyalty to himself.

The Secret Warning

The missing detail of the oath helps to explain not only how Amleth's foster brother can work as a trusted agent of his enemy but also why he does not communicate with Amleth directly. When he warns Amleth to beware of treachery, he does so, not straightforwardly, which would be an abuse of his sworn word, but indirectly, so that strictly he does not violate his oath. That is, the message is transmitted nonverbally not so much to conceal it from the other henchmen as to enable the foster brother to observe the word, if not the spirit, of his oath. The interpretation also finds support externally. When Regin wishes to help his foster sons Hroar and Helgi but will not talk with them in order not to break his oath to King Froði, he rides his horse back and forth between the boys and Froði's hall, while gesturing in such a way as to suggest anger and fighting. The boys finally understand that he is trying to communicate with them without violating his oath, so that they follow him towards the king's hall. When they reach some trees, Regin says, as though to himself, "If I had a great grievance against King Froði, I would set fire to these trees." The boys perceive that he wants them to set fire to the hall, and they do so. In this story it is explicitly said that the foster father adopts indirect means of communication in order not to break his oath. Regin gestures nonverbally, and when he does speak he pretends to be speaking to himself and even so speaks indirectly, referring to the king's hall metaphorically as "these trees." So also Amleth's foster brother helps him with a message that is not only secret, because of the presence of Fengi's men, but also indirect, because of his own oath to Fengi.

That brings us to the message itself, a gadfly with a straw embedded in its back. I am not entirely sure that anyone has managed to break the code, but Jørgen Olrik has given us the best explanation so far offered. He suggests that the message takes the form of a rebus for Danish *agnbak* 'straw-back' or 'chaff-back', evidently an old nickname for a kind of petty thief who stole grain from the sheaves of the field during the night and betrayed himself by the chaff that clung to his back. The penalty given the *agnbak* was severe. The meaning of the message is then more or less this: "Don't be as stupid as the grain thief, the straw-back, who betrays himself against his will, and take care that you don't share his fate."[20]

Sperber disagrees with Olrik's contention that the gadfly itself has no significance in the message, but his own solution is too difficult. He argues that the communication is made up of the elements *agn* 'straw', for which there was an Old Danish homonym *avn* 'bait', and Old Icelandic *fluga*, which means literally "fly" and figuratively "bait." Both elements of the message therefore signify "bait."[21] Sperber overlooks the fact that the insect mentioned by Saxo is not simply a fly but a gadfly. I fear moreover that if one part of the message were in Old Danish and the other part in Old Icelandic, Amleth might have continued to ponder the puzzle long after everyone else gave up the test and returned home.

Finally, Geoffrey Bullough's solution, if not especially plausible, has at least the virtue of simplicity. He believes that the message warns Amleth to beware of "the sting in the woman's tail."[22]

Amleth's Bed

Back in the hall Amleth acknowledges that he lay with the girl. When the men ask him what he used as a cushion, he tells them that he lay on an animal's hoof, a cock's comb, and some roof beams ("ungulae iumenti, cristaeque galli, laquearibus quoque tecti innixum dixit"). Saxo adds that to avoid lying Amleth gathered pieces of each of these materials when he was setting out for the bog with the girl. Like the king's men, however, Saxo takes Amleth literally here and misses the point. "Horsehoof" and "cockscomb," as Axel Olrik observes, are the popular names of certain plants both in Denmark and elsewhere, and if these are actually plants, then the roof beams are probably a translation of Danish *tagrør* 'reed', literally "roof-reed."[23] Since all three plants are commonly found in marshes and meadows, they would have been at hand in the bog to which Amleth brought the girl, so that he did not need to gather "pieces of all these things" beforehand, as Saxo has him do. Not understanding the puns, Saxo tries to explain how the youth happens to be in possession of such unlikely articles as a hoof and a cock's comb. In the usual oral telling of this incident, Amleth was perhaps made to say simply that he lay on a *hestehov* 'horsehoof', *hanekam* 'cockscomb', and *tag* 'roof /thatch'. *Tag* is both the ordinary Danish word for "roof" and also a very old word for "thatch," that is, any plant used for roofing, especially reed.[24]

A. Nordfelt, however, suggests that Saxo had an Anglo-Saxon source for this incident in which the plant names had the form of three alliterating pairs: "horses hōf," "coccs comb," and "(h)rōfs rūde" ("roof's rue"). Saxo, not understanding that Anglo-Saxon *rūde* was the name of the plant "rue," incorrectly connected *hrōfs rūde* with Danish *rude* 'quadrangular plane' and thus took the phrase to refer to a roof patterned with quadrangles; consequently, he rendered the phrase in Latin by "laquearia tecti," which strictly means a "paneled ceiling," that is, a surface composed of crisscrossed beams or the like, making a pattern of recessed quadrangular hollows.[25] Despite the ingenuity of Nordfelt's solution, the objections to it are fatal. There is no certain trace of the Hamlet story outside of Denmark and Iceland. Apart from that, the supposition that Saxo drew upon an Anglo-Saxon source here is certainly more difficult than that he drew upon a Scandinavian source. And the phrase "hrōfs rūde" allows of no sensible pun comparable to those on "horsehoof" and "cockscomb". Finally, so far as I know, Saxo was no more likely to interpret Anglo-Saxon *rūde* 'rue' as "quadrangular plane" than as "rue," since *rude* was also the Danish word for "rue."[26] It is therefore easier to understand Saxo's phrase "laquearia tecti" as an attempt to render Danish *tagrør*.

Conclusion

The first test concludes with a brief exchange between Amleth and his foster brother in the hall and has to do with the fact that

Amleth does not know who sent him the secret warning. His benefactor, wishing to inform him of his service, remarks, "I have been singularly devoted to you recently." By way of acknowledgement Amleth replies: "I did in fact notice something suddenly flit by with a stalk of chaff clinging to its rear end." The foster brother knows that the "something" refers to the insect, while the bystanders believe that it refers to the foster brother and so miss the point.

5. The Second Test

As in the first test, Saxo does not explain clearly how the test itself is arranged, leading one to conclude once more that the events presuppose a fuller and more coherent version of the story than that which Saxo presents. In the present instance it is unclear, first, why Fengi chooses to make a show of departure and, second, why the eavesdropper can expect to find mother and son together in Geruth's room at a certain time. These problems disappear, however, if we assume that Amleth, like Ambales, sleeps regularly in his mother's room. The eavesdropper therefore knows that Geruth and Amleth can be found together in Geruth's room each evening, and the purpose of Fengi's departure is to permit mother and son to be there alone. The scene accordingly takes place at night when the members of the household, including the queen and her son, have retired for the evening. The nocturnal setting explains in turn how Amleth can so casually cut a man up, cook him, and take him outside to the outhouse, all as though no one else were around.

The Eavesdropper

Fengi's friend sneaks into the bedroom and hides under the straw.[27] Straw or other vegetation was sometimes strewn upon the floor, even in a royal house, especially during festive occasions. But Saxo is more likely thinking of bed straw, whether he imagines the queen's room furnished with mere piles of straw on the ground or with freestanding beds. A man wishing to conceal himself would find no spot more ideal for the purpose than a medieval freestanding bed, which was simply a man-sized box on four legs, filled deeply with straw. Fengi's unoccupied sleeping place is presumably available for the intruder's use. In the *Ambales Saga* the spy hides *under* one of the beds in Amba's room.

The outdoor facility through and under which the eavesdropper meets his ignoble end is obviously situated, not over a hole in the earth in the more familiar manner, but simply above the flat ground, either in the pig sty or in an open yard, where the swine have an opportunity of sifting through the human refuse for nourishment.[28]

6. The Third Test

In the third test the trial concerns, not the hero's disguise, but his life. The principal difficulty for Saxo's reader lies in making sense of Amleth's puzzling behavior at the royal dinner in Britain.

The Polluted Feast

Both the main lines and the details of this episode are recognizable as an international folktale.[29] Amleth shows exceptional sensitivity in the present adventure and nowhere else because he assumes here the role of the perceptive folktale hero. Originally independent, the story has been adapted to the Danish legend, though, the reader may feel, with some inconsistency, since the marvelous abilities that Amleth displays for a time are strictly not of the same order as those which he has exibited heretofore. Extraordinary cunning and resourcefulness do not imply an almost supernaturally keen sensitivity to food and drink and superhuman powers of deduction. A couple of examples will suffice to illustrate the tale type and to clarify the problems in Saxo's narrative.

The tale of the *Three Vagabonds*, told in *The Thousand and One Nights,*[30] concerns three impoverished men who decide to go to the sultan and say that each of them is the master of an art. They go to the palace, where one tells the sultan that he is a jeweler, the second that he knows about horses, and the third that he knows about people. The sultan decides to keep them there to test them. He asks the first man to evaluate a certain clear jewel in his possession. After studying it closely the man says that it has a worm in it. The sultan breaks the jewel, finds that it is true, and asks the vagabond how he knew it, to which the man answers, "By the sharpness of my sight." The sultan sends him back to his comrades with bread and soup. Later he asks the second vagabond to evaluate a beautiful black foal. After testing it the man declares that it excels all others except for one fault – its mother was a buffalo cow. The sultan confirms this charge by consulting the former owner of the animal, and then asks the vagabond how he discerned the fact. The man explains that the hoof of a horse is round, whereas that of a buffalo is cloven and oblong. Satisfied, the sultan orders him to be given soup and bread. Remembering that the third vagabond claimed to be a judge of people, the sultan bids him test his wife, and the man, after a long examination, reports that she has only one fault: her mother was a dancer. The sultan confirms this by consulting his wife's father, and asks the vagabond how he deduced the matter. The man replies that dancers have slit eyes and their eyelids are turned upwards. The sultan has him served soup and bread. When the sultan then asks the same man to tell him of his own descent, the man says the sultan is a child of sin and adultery. Sword in hand he goes to his mother and demands the truth, and she confesses that she had seduced the cook, whose son he is. After turning over his rule to the third vagabond, the sultan asks him how he deduced his descent. The man explains that after each session the sultan ordered soup and bread to be brought to them; from that he recognized that the ruler was the son of the cook, for kings are wont to give money and gifts.

The tale of *The Clever Students* was collected in the last century from a woman in western Jutland.[31] Each of three students is a connoisseur of food, drink, or people. Passing the night at a certain gentleman's house, one will not touch the meat during the evening meal, the second refuses the wine, and the third will not drink with their host. Later the host stands at their door and eavesdrops on their conversation, hearing that one did not want to eat dog flesh, the other did not wish to drink wine that had the taste of a corpse, and the third did not care to drink with a bastard. The host learns the truth from his servants and his mother, and sends the students on their way with gifts.

In these stories three men visit a man of high standing (sultan / gentleman / king). The three guests (vagabonds / students) each possess an extraordinary skill, or one of the three (Amleth) has several skills. In the Jutish folktale as in the Amleth legend the meat and drink are refused, and so the host is led to eavesdrop upon the private conversation of his guests. In the Arabian tale the sultan's wife proves to be of low birth, as does the queen in the Danish legend. In all three stories it is revealed that the host is a bastard. The clues lie in the nature of the person's eyes (the sultana's slit eyes / the king's thrallish eyes) or in their lowly habits (the sultan behaves like a cook / the queen acts like a servant).[32] After confirming the several charges made by his guests, the sultan turns over his sultanate to one of them; the Danish gentleman sends the students off with gifts; the British king gives Amleth his daughter in marriage. It is obvious enough that these are different developments of essentially the same tale, and that Amleth owes his marvelous, though temporary, sensitivity to impurities to his being assigned the role of the perceptive guest of the folktale.

One problem remains to be explained. Amleth's statements are founded upon an unusually fine sense of taste and smell and upon close attention to details of appearance and behavior. He describes what he perceives, and his host the king verifies the perceptions. Or rather, the king verifies all but two of them. In a variant motif reported by Saxo, Amleth finds fault with the mead for tasting of a corpse, for (Amleth says) the bees fed upon the paunch of a corpse and transferred the flavor to their honeycombs. But how can he deduce their history from the flavor of the mead? He cannot, nor is the king said to verify it. In the other instance Amleth reveals not only that the queen's mother was a thrall but also that she came into her condition of servitude as a result of being captured in war. Can the queen's lowly habits really reveal all this? Hardly. These illogicalities arose at some point in the transmission of the legend when a storyteller – Saxo or a predecessor – unthinkingly transferred to Amleth observations that properly belonged to the king. It is Amleth's role to deduce that the mead has been polluted with the flavor of death and that the queen's parent was a thrall. It is then his host's part to discover, upon investigation, the historical details that verify the deductions: the bees fed upon the paunch of a dead man, and the queen's mother was taken prisoner of war and – literally – enthralled. After careless storytelling has taken these statements from the host and given them to the guest, Amleth's powers, already extraordinary, become explicable to the more reflective reader only on the assumption that they are somehow preternatural. This is exactly the conclusion to which Belleforest was forced, with great effect on the subsequent literary development of the Hamlet story.[33]

The Gold-filled Sticks

When the Danes ask Amleth about his missing escorts, he holds forth his two gold-filled sticks and says, "Here they are, both of them." The grim jest is familiar from the sagas, in which the aggrieved party sometimes identifies blood money with the dead man. When, for example, Grettir kills Björn, the dead man's brother declares that he will not carry his brother in a money-bag; that is, he will not take wergild in place of revenge.[34] In exactly the same sense Amleth refers to the hidden gold as his companions. He could have shown the Danes a money-bag instead, but then he would have betrayed himself, since the point would have been appreciated immediately.[35]

7. Amleth's Revenge

The Funeral

Amleth's plan is to trap his enemies in a sort of giant shroud and cremate them. A funeral offers several advantages that are crucial to his unusual strategy. The most obvious is that Fengi and his men will be conveniently assembled in one place, the royal hall. A hall was essentially a large gathering-room, built to hold many men for days of eating and drinking. Rectangular in shape, it embraced an oblong hearth in its center, to the warmth and light of which everything in the room was oriented. Fixed benches lined at least the two long walls, and tables stood before them.

During a funeral celebration, moreover, no one would find it remarkable that hangings clothed the walls. These precious textiles would normally be kept in storage, protected from the humidity and the smoke, but they would be taken out and hung up on special occasions to give the otherwise bare hall a festive appearance, though for funerals the hangings were possibily grey or black. A hanging was a horizontal strip of woven or embroidered cloth, less than a yard high and often very long. Since the hall had no windows or obstructing furniture, a single hanging or several sewn together could trail around all four walls without hindrance, filling more or less the narrow space available between the top of the low walls and the heads of those seated on the benches. The presence of hangings, then, was a normal feature of a funeral in the hall of a well-to-do family.[36]

Finally, the celebrants will imbibe heavily, for drinking was almost the one essential activity of the old funeral practice. Men honored the deceased by drinking his funeral ale. Saxo tells the tale (1.8.27) of Hunding, king of the Swedes, who receives false tidings of the death of King Hadding of Denmark, and holds a funeral in his honor. He fills an immense vessel with ale and has it placed in the midst of the guests, to their delight. He even acts as server, but as he goes about in the hall pouring the drink, he stumbles, falls into the vessel, and drowns in the ale. King Hadding, hearing of this and wishing to pay Hunding a like honor, publicly hangs himself. Like Hunding, Amleth plays the cup-bearer, plying the men liberally with drink.

Fengi's Death

In slaying Fengi, Amleth observes the etiquette of the Old Scandinavian killer. His procedure here can be contrasted with that of Rosemund and her helper in the Lombard legend of the murder of Alboin, related in the eighth century by Paul the Deacon.[37] Alboin, king of the Lombards, kills King Cunimund in battle and weds his daughter Rosemund. He has a drinking goblet made of Cunimund's head. One day while Alboin sits merrily at a banquet, he orders the goblet to be filled and passed to the queen, inviting her to drink with her father. Not amused, Rosemund determines to avenge her father. While Alboin naps, she binds his sword tightly to the head of his bed so that it can be neither removed nor drawn, and then lets into the room a fellow conspirator to finish him off. Alboin awakens, tries in vain to draw his sword, and is slain.

In both the Lombard and the Danish forms of this story, narrative economy dictates that the victim wake up before the assassin strikes so that he may try unsuccessfully to draw his weapon; otherwise, there is little point in introducing the motif of the bound sword. But only in the Danish version does the killer intentionally rouse his victim before finishing him off. A Scandinavian regarded it as proper to wake a sleeping adversary before attacking him, although he did not feel obliged to give the man any real chance to defend himself.[38]

8. The Aftermath

The Succession

From the viewpoint of the national monarch, the kingship of Jutland is an appointive office. But Amleth appeals to the principle of election, the old custom according to which certain freeman have the right to elect, or at least to confirm by acclamation, their future king. Amleth bids the Jutes acclaim him king, they do so, and he is king of Jutland. Though in his speech he calls himself the "lawful successor" to the throne, he does not mean that the office automatically passes by inheritance from father to son, which would imply a third principle of succession. Rather, he is alluding to the fact that candidates for the kingship were customarily limited to persons of royal blood. With his father and uncle dead, he is the only obvious candidate.

9. The King of Britain

The Continuation of the Story

To the extent that the Amleth legend is biographical in form, it should now require little more than a notice of the hero's death to give it an ending. Instead of that, however, two additional tales intervene between the hero's present elevation and his eventual death. Compared with the initial adventure, the continuation is markedly inferior in narrative excitement and dramatic interest. The same can be said of the continuations in the legends of H and H and of Brutus: they are less memorable than the particular form of the Hero as Fool that precedes them.

It emerges first that Amleth's revenge is incomplete, for a close ally of Fengi survives. The second story replicates the theme of personal revenge that dominates the first story, with the king of Britain now replacing Fengi as Amleth's adversary. Like his predecessor, he sends the hero off to be slain by another's hand, but the hero escapes his intended fate and returns to slay the king. The revenge has finally been pursued to its end. Fengi and all his allies have been exterminated.

The third tale picks up another theme of the first story, the assumption of political office. At the beginning of the legend, King Rørik of Denmark appoints Ørvendil and Fengi to their office in Jutland. Fengi murders his brother and for a while enjoys an unshared throne. Amleth in turn kills Fengi and bids the Jutes acclaim him king, which they do. Now the new king of the land, Viglek, challenges Amleth's right to the throne, since he regards such appointments as the prerogative of the national ruler. Amleth loses life, wife, and throne to Viglek.

The final two tales, then, follow causally from the first and explore the implications of the hero's final actions in that story, taking each of the two actions in the order of their original occurrence. The second story revives the revenge theme, simply replacing Fengi with his blood brother, who continues Fengi's policy of attempting to do away with Amleth, as though Fengi had come back to life. It sustains the verdict of the initial story, which is that Amleth's vengeance is justified, for the second tale does little else than restate the contention of Amleth and Fengi in another way. But the third story overturns the verdict of the first with regard to Amleth's accession to the kingship. It reexamines the theme of the awarding of political office, replacing the Jutes with King Viglek. The final stories restate two important themes in their predecessor and serve to strengthen or weaken the features they expand upon, qualifying the propositions acted out in the initial adventure. They affirm the right of the individual to assert himself aggressively in the sphere of personal revenge, to maintain the honor and integrity of the family without regard to the cost in lives, provided there is good cause. But they question or deny the right of personal initiative and individual aggression in the realm of political power, which may threaten the integrity of the polity.[39] In short, two varieties of personal aggression are distinguished and opposed in the continuation of the narrative.

The Oath

Fengi and the king of Britain once swore a mutual pact that the survivor would avenge the other's death. The implication, as Saxo's countrymen would readily understand, is that the two men are sworn brothers, or blood brothers.[40] Notice that in the *Ambales Saga* the two corresponding monarchs, Faustinus and Tamerlaus, are half brothers.

Herminthrud

The strategy adopted by the British king is virtually the same as that employed earlier by Fengi. Each king dispatches the youth to a foreign monarch, together with a letter that should induce the recipient to put Amleth to death. But while the bearer of the letter sleeps, the message is changed so that the hero, instead of perishing, weds the princess or the queen.[41] Then he returns and kills the king who sent him. Both episodes are inspired by the same international folktale,[42] in which an evil king makes repeated attempts to do away with a poor youth in an unsuccessful effort to avoid the fulfillment of a prophecy that the boy will become the king's son-in-law. Saxo evidently tries to account for the obvious similarities between the two adventures in his narrative by having Amleth's illustrated shield suggest to the queen of Scotland the trick of rewriting the letter.

The telling of the story lacks some clarity. If Amleth is aware from the start, as he seems to be, that his mission is to act as go-between for the king of Britain, it is hard to understand how he is deceived by the letter that Herminthrud reads in his presence. But if he is not deceived, there is little point in a counterfeit letter at all, since there is no one else to fool. Later he tries without success to convince the king of Britain that Herminthrud and her scout did in fact trick him.

If, moreover, it is Herminthrud's custom to kill her suitors, would it not be more effective for the king of Britain to send Amleth with a letter which, unknown to Amleth, represented him rather than the king of Britain as a suitor? But then there would of course be no need of the incident in which Amleth's letter was rewritten. A simpler solution would be to present the queen as an executor of her suitors and of their messengers as well. Perhaps that is to be understood. In any case, the folktale is imperfectly adapted to the larger story and is less coherent than the earlier adaptation.

10. King Viglek

Fjaller

Amleth drives out a certain Jarl Fjaller of Skaane, and "the story goes that he fled to a place called Undensakre, which is unknown to my people." Saxo seems to have misunderstood a poetic or mythological statement that in effect meant "Fjaller perished."[43] It is not clear, however, what Fjaller has to do with the story, and one must suppose that if he really belonged to it, the connection either was lost to Saxo or has dropped out of the text.

Amleth's Grave

Saxo says that there is a field in Jutland that contains Amleth's barrow and is named after him. Very likely he is referring to Ammelhede, south of Randers Fjord in eastern Jutland. Ammelhede (that is, Ammel Heath) answers nicely to the field in Jutland bearing Amleth's name, since *Ammel* could be a corruption of an old form of Amleth's name (though it need not be) and there are still remains of an ancient barrow there. In the last century a local legend was told about a king who was supposed to lie in it.

> There lived two petty kings over by Virring, a half-mile north of here, and something came between them, and they slew each other. One was called Ammel and lived over by Ammelhede; he lies buried in a little mound just east of there. The other was called Krog and lived in Krogsgaard.[44]

But the story need not be very old.

Although there may have been a popular tradition in medieval times associating the hero's grave with Ammelhede, it appears just as likely that the connection has been wrought by a succession of learned etymologists. According to *The Annals of Ryd,* a Danish source that is roughly contemporary with Saxo's *History of the Danes* (see Appendix I), Amleth perishes, not on land, but in a sea battle in Øresund, the sound between Zealand and Skaane. Saxo, however, has Amleth win an initial victory against Viglek in Zealand and Skaane, and then rather suddenly reappear in Jutland to do battle again and die.[45] It is possible that Saxo knew of Ammelhede in Jutland, inferred that the Jutish hero lay buried there, and changed the site of the final battle in his narrative from Øresund to Jutland in order to be able to include a notice of Amleth's burial place at Ammelhede.[46]

If so, Saxo was merely one of a number of learned Danes who, rightly or wrongly, have seen Amleth's name embedded in Ammelhede.[47] In 1575 Saxo's first translator, Anders Vedel, probably had the place in mind when he rendered Saxo's Latin rather freely: "The field in Jutland where he was buried is still called after his name Amlet's Hede." In the early 1600s Anne Krabbe noted in her manuscript of *The Danish Rhyme Chronicle* that Amleth "lies buried out in Ambleth Hede, which lies by Estrup." She herself lived just ten kilometers north of Ammelhede, whose name she treats with some liberty here. In 1858 Saxo's commentators Müller and Velschow cite in this connection Amelhede (*sic*) near Randers.[48] And in 1933 local enthusiasm was responsible for the raising of a new stone on the ancient grave. It bears a metrical inscription composed by Jørgen Olrik:

AMLETH — ANTIQUITY'S
FINEST GENIUS —
PLAYED THE FOOL
TILL THE HOUR OF REVENGE —
CHOSEN KING
BY THE JUTES IN ASSEMBLY —
SET IN A BARROW HE RESTS
AT AMMELHEDE — .[49]

Appendix I: Hamlet in Danish Annals and Chronicles

In addition to Saxo's, five other early Danish accounts of Hamlet have come down to us.[1] Like his, they are parts of larger historical works, for it was as a figure of Danish history that Hamlet interested learned Danes, and not as a character of imaginative fiction. These accounts are the only other native sources for the legend, the only other evidence we have for the life of the story in Danish oral tradition. They also provide some indication of how Saxo's learned countrymen actually read his treatment of the Hamlet story.

Annals and chronicles from Danish monasteries first appeared in the twelfth century and continued being composed in different parts of the kingdom for about three hundred years. In the fourteenth century men began to translate these little Latin works into Danish so that laymen might also be able to read the accounts of the kings and heroes of old. The forms of the characters' names differ considerably, and I have let them stand here as they appear in the manuscripts, except that I have dropped the inflectional endings of Latinized names. The composers of these humble works drew freely from Saxo, from one another, and from other sources that have since disappeared. The products of their labors are brief and unimaginative, frequently confused, and sometimes outright absurd.

The Annals of Ryd was composed in Latin around the middle of the thirteenth century by a Cistercian monk at Ryd Monastery by Flensborg

Fjord in southern Jutland. It is therefore a product of Saxo's own century. A king list preceding the annals proper catalogs the kings of Denmark, who are numbered in succession. Hamlet is here Danish king number 26. One or two remarks follow each name.

> 23. Rørik. Orwendæl succeeded him.
>
> 24. Orwendæl. This man was very successful in battle and performed many outstanding deeds. His brother Foggi slew him and reigned.
>
> 25. Foggi. He took for himself the wife of the brother he slew. Amblet, son of said Orwændæl, slew him to avenge his father, and he burnt up with him all the nobles in the kingdom together with the entire royal house such that there was not one survivor.
>
> 26. Amblet, who was a very clever man, slew the king of England in war and gained control of Denmark, England, and Scotland. King Wichlech of Norway, his stepfather, slew him in battle in Øresund, and reigned.
>
> 27. Wichlech. He took Amblet's wife after divorcing his own.

The Annals of Slesvig came into being shortly after the foregoing annals (the last annalistic entry is for the year 1268) in southern Jutland. The work is also preceded by a king list, in which Hamlet is Danish king number 28.

> 25. Rorick Slengeboge. He was king in Skaane and the islands. In his time Orwalder and Feggo were kings in Jutland.
>
> 27. Feggi, who slew his brother and became king of all Denmark. He was slain together with all his court at Viborg.
>
> 28. Anlet, son of Oruældær, is slain.

The Runic Chronicle was composed early in the fourteenth century, probably by a monk at a monastery in northern Skaane in eastern Denmark. It is written in Danish in runes. The chronicle is the work of a short-lived school of writing in which runes were taken into use for book writing.

> Then Roþrik, Høþþær's son, was king. In his time there lived Slænge and Uækæ, and Oruændæn slew Slænge, and Ambluþe

in turn slew him. They were kings in Jutland. And his brother-in-law was named Uiþlek.

The History of the Danes in Danish was probably composed shortly after *The Runic Chronicle*, at Lund in Skaane, where the writer had access to materials kept in the Lund Cathedral and where there was some continuity of historical work. This and the following text are from manuscripts copied in the fifteenth century.

Then Rørik Slængeborræ was king. Then his son Rake was king. He conquered Curland, the Wends, and Sweden. They refused him tribute. He made Ørwændæl and Fæng rulers in Jutland. The king gave Ørwændæl his sister because of his success. He begot with her a son, and he was called Ambløthæ. Afterwards Fæng killed Ørwældæl out of envy, and wed his wife.

Then Ambløthæ feared for his life and played the fool. Fæng suspected Ambløtæ and sent him to the king of Britain with two of his housecarls and a letter to the effect that Ambløthæ should be hanged. He scraped that off while they were sleeping, and wrote that the two housecarls should be hanged and that Amblothæ should have the king's daughter. And so it happened. One year later, when Fæng was celebrating Ambløthæ's funeral, he came to Denmark and killed Fæng his father's slayer, and burnt all Fæng's men inside of a hanging, and became king of Jutland. Later he went back to Britain and killed his father-in-law, who wanted to avenge Fæng's death. Then he wed the queen of Scotland. As soon as he came home, he was slain in battle.

After Rørik Rake, his son Wighlek was king. His queen was named Nanna. He had peace and quiet in his days, and he later died a natural death.

Composed in Danish, *The Legend Chronicle* gives a free retelling of the careers of Denmark's first sixty-five monarchs. Its account of Hamlet is the youngest and the longest of the minor lives of Hamlet.

The twenty-second king was Rørik Slengæbuk, and he was king in Skaane, Ærø, Falster, Møn, Taasinge, and Lolland, and in his days there were two kings, one in Jutland and one in Zealand.

The twenty-third king was Ornwalder and his brother Faggæ. Then Faggæ slew his brother Ornwalder because he wanted to reign alone in the kingdom.

The twenty-fourth king was Faggæ. He was king over all Denmark. He wed the same wife as his brother had had before. She had a son named Amlæd with King Ornwalder. This same Amlæd came to Viborg, and he encountered there King Fæggæ, his own uncle. He set fire to Viborg and burnt up the entire royal estate, burning up the king inside of it and with him many noble men, and thus he avenged his father's death and then became king after him.

The twenty-fifth king was Amlæd, King Ornwalder's son. He was a very clever king. He slew King Fæggæ in Denmark, and slew the king of England and the king of Scotland in a battle in England, and wed an English maiden whose name was Ingæfreth. She was the daughter of the king of England and ruled all England after her father was slain. He brought her to Denmark with him and ruled over all Denmark, England, and Scotland. Then he began to quarrel with his brother-in-law, the king of Norway, who was wed to his sister. He wanted to have Norway in addition to that which he already held in good peace. When the king of Norway understood that he might not enjoy his kingdom in peace, he summoned all Norsemen to meet the king of Denmark in Øresund. There he slew King Amlæd and many good Danes with him, and the kingdom suffered great harm. But before the Norsemen got away from Denmark after doing that damage, Queen Ingæfred pursued them with as many men as she could collect and slew them all, both the king and others whom she could get hold of, and avenged her husband very honorably.

Since the chroniclers' works are structured as summary notices of the careers of Denmark's successive monarchs, it was crucial for the composers to determine just who were the rulers of the realm. The compiler of *The Annals of Ryd* conceives of Ørvendil, Fengi, and Amleth as kings of all Denmark rather than of Jutland only, as Saxo does. Rørik is succeeded by Ørvendil, who is succeeded by his brother Fengi, who is followed in turn by Amleth and then by Viglek. There is probably some local patriotism here. Saxo, who was probably a Zealander and in any case has a bias in favor of Zealand, makes Ørvendil, Fengi, and Amleth to be Jutish subordinates of the Zealand monarchs, whereas the Jutish annalist gives them coordinate status.

The two traditions of the monarchy represented in Saxo's *Gesta Danorum* and in *The Annals of Ryd*, both of them influential works in Danish historiography, plagued subsequent writers, who had either to prefer the one to the other or to try to reconcile the conflicting traditions. The compiler of *The Annals of Slesvig* makes Rørik king of eastern Denmark and gives Jutland two simultaneous rulers, as in Saxo. Though he does not say that the western kings are subordinate to the eastern king, only Rørik, king number 25, is numbered as a king of Denmark. But Ørvendil (who is obviously the missing king number 26) must somehow become king of all Denmark upon Rørik's death, since Fengi later succeeds Ørvendil as king of the land. The monk tries to synthesize the two traditions by making first the one and then the other of the Jutland kings become Zealand kings, but the Jutland tradition reasserts itself when King Fengi of Denmark is said to be slain at Viborg, long the most important town in Jutland. The writer imagines Fengi as residing there, which would be natural if he were the regional monarch. *The Runic Chronicle* and *The History of the Danes in Danish* follow the tradition known to Saxo, but *The Legend Chronicle*, like *The Annals of Slesvig*, combines the two traditions of the kingship. Rørik is king of eastern Denmark, while Jutland is ruled by another monarch, who is unnamed. Nevertheless, Ørvendil, Fengi, and Amleth are each in their turn kings of all the land. The traditions are combined with some sleight of hand: Rørik is succeeded by both Ørvendil and Fengi, who together are the twenty-fourth king of Denmark. But Fengi again meets his slayer in Viborg just as though he were a Jutish king.

Names were also a source of confusion. The author of *The Runic Chronicle* mentions that during the reign of Rørik "there lived Slænge and Uækæ, and Oruændæn slew Slænge." The two interlopers Slænge and Uækæ seem to have come into being as the result of a misinterpretation of one of Rørik's nicknames, Ring-Slinger, spelled variously as "Slengeboge," "Slængborræ," "Slengæbuk," and so forth. The chronicler seems also to reverse victim and villain when he reports that Oruændæn (that is, Ørvendil) slew Slænge (that is, Fengi?). The copyist of *The History of the Danes in Danish* similarly trips on Rake, another nickname of Rørik. Initially he makes Rake the son and successor of Rørik.

Then Rørik Slængeborræ was king. Then his son Rake was king. In the end the son vanishes as quickly as he came into being, and the nickname is back in place after Rørik's name.

> After Rørik Rake, his son Wighlek was king.

The correct sense is preserved in another manuscript.

> Then Rozik Slangeboræ or Rakæ, his son, was king.[2]

Rozik (that is, Rørik) is here introduced as the son of the preceding monarch, but to one ignorant of Rørik's second nickname it appears as though he had a son named "Rakæ."

The compilers were usually content to record little more than the beginning and end of the monarch's reigns, so the narratives are skeletal. A few details appear that are not mentioned in Saxo or conflict with his account. A couple of the chronicles locate the royal residence in Viborg in Jutland. One of them honors Amleth's first wife with a name. We hear rather more about Viglek than Saxo relates, such as that he was Rørik's son, that he was the king of Norway, that he was wed to Amleth's sister or to the twice-widowed Geruth, that he was content to remain with his own wife Nanna rather than to take Amleth's Scots spouse, or that he was slain by Amleth's English bride, who, unlike Saxo's faithless Herminthrud, bravely avenged the death of her husband. Two of the sources report that Amleth's last battle with Viglek took place in Øresund, so that perhaps Amleth had a watery grave. All in all, the harvest of new information is small. It is not clear whether the variations are due more to popular or to learned tradition, but the difference is hardly important. Perhaps more than anything else the documents illustrate the relative poverty of the written tradition after Saxo.

In Saxo's day one could still hear stories of the ancient rulers of Denmark, but one by one the old traditions were passing into oblivion. The legend of Hamlet was no exception. The story did not live forever on the lips of the Jutes and other Danes, and there must have come a day when it was told for the last time. Saxo drew directly or indirectly on oral tradition; his immediate successors drew upon the works of their predecessors, on works that no longer survive, and perhaps on oral informants. *The Legend Chronicle* did not mark the end of Danish Hamlets, but no subsequent treatments of the hero seem to draw either on oral tradition or on written sources unknown to us. Either the legend had died out or there came into being a cleavage between the oral storyteller and the literary man.

Appendix II: The First Hamlet Illustrations

The sixteenth century was a period of national sentiment in Europe. For Denmark it was the century in which Saxo's work was first printed (1514) and translated (1575), and although plans for a new Danish history in Latin did not get very far, at least two artists are known to have painted pictures of Denmark's legendary and historical kings.[1] In Sweden, Johannes Magnus wrote *The History of All the Kings of the Goths and Swedes*, in which he was able to mention no fewer than 143 Swedish kings.[2] There were more monarchs than Denmark could boast, and they went further back, the first being Noah's son Japheth. The king of Sweden ordered a series of tapestries to be made, portraying these noble rulers. Although the project was never completed, he seems to have given his Danish rival the same idea. Frederik II contracted with his court painter, Hans Knieper of Antwerp, to make a splendid series of wool and silk tapestries for Kronborg's Great Hall. They were to portray the king, his son Christian, and his precdecessors on the throne. Above each king was to be the period of his reign, how he fared, and what end he met; under his feet there were to be his extraction and the arms of the kingdom. The Danish king settled for 113 kings against the Swedes' 143; the oldest Danish monarch, Dan, was merely a contemporary of David. Woven at Elsinore in 1581–86, the Kronborg tapestries provided an illustrated history of the kingship. Evidently 100 kings were represented on forty tapestries, some of the tapestries showing more than 1 monarch.[3] Like the hangings of earlier days, woven tapestries were precious possessions that were ordinarily kept in storage, but taken out and hung up on special occasions to give a festive appearance to bare rooms or royal tents. Fourteen of the tapestries survive, of which seven still hang in Kronborg.

For the purpose of the tapestry series, Frederik had to decide just who his predecessors were. If he accepted Saxo as his guide, Hamlet (among others) was excluded, since he was merely a regional king. If Frederik chose to follow *The Annals of Ryd* or *The Danish Rhyme Chronicle,*[4] Hamlet was included as a national monarch. As it turned out, Frederik preferred Saxo's recently translated work, so Hamlet was omitted.[5] Ironically, neither he nor his father or uncle hung in image in the castle at Elsinore with which they became so firmly associated at a later date. But the famed tapestries did play a part in inspiring, directly or indirectly, a number of illustrated manuscripts in which the kings of Denmark were portrayed in likeness. Dating from the end of the sixteenth to the middle of the following century, these were illustrated Danish histories that belonged to wealthy families. Whereas some of them, like the tapestries, follow the semiofficial list of kings in Saxo, others draw also on *The Danish Rhyme Chronicle* and therefore take in additional kings. The latter group contains the earliest surviving pictures of Hamlet.

The two oldest pictures are in color. One of these (fig. 1) appears in a manuscript that belonged to Anne Krabbe, who died in 1618. Amblett, as he is called here, stands in a conventional royal pose with the symbols of dominion, the scepter and the orb, the latter almost suggesting the head of Yorick. The heading comes from *The Danish Rhyme Chronicle*, with some additions.

> Amblett, Rørik's daughter's son, king of Denmark. He played the fool and later became a powerful king and got the queen of Scotland, who was named Hermedrude. He became king in the year 3507 B.C. and reigned for sixty-five years.

Although all the likenesses of Hamlet ultimately rest only upon the authority of the artist's imaginations, this clean-shaven Hamlet is something of a fraud, for he is merely a copy of King Dan from another manuscript.[6]

The other (fig. 2) shows a rather sporting Hamlet, with mustache and beard and flowing locks. He holds an orb in his left hand and grips a sword rather than a scepter in his right. Above him is a scroll reading "Amblet Rørigs Dattersøn." The book belonged to Anne Krabbe's cousin Karen Skram, who added: "This king played the fool and then became a powerful king."[7]

The remaining two illustrations (figs. 3 and 4) are drawn in ink without color.[8]

Figure 1. *Amblett. Probably the oldest picture of Hamlet. Courtesy of the Royal Library, Copenhagen*

Figure 2. *Amblet. From a manuscript dated 1597. Courtesy of the Royal Library, Stockholm*

Figure 3. *Amlets. From a manuscript written before* 1638.
Courtesy of the Royal Library, Copenhagen

Figure 4. *Amlets. From a manuscript dated 1658. Courtesy of the Royal Library, Copenhagen*

Abbreviations

Aarne-Thompson
Antti Aarne and Stith Thompson, *The Types of the Folktale: A Classification and Bibliography.*

Detter
Ferd. Detter, "Die Hamletssage," *Zeitschrift für deutsches Altertum und deutsche Litteratur* 36 (1892): 1–25.

Dollerup
Cay Dollerup, *Denmark, "Hamlet," and Shakespeare: A Study of Englishmen's Knowledge of Denmark towards the End of the Sixteenth Century with Special Reference to "Hamlet."*

Elton & Powell
Oliver Elton, trans., and Frederick York Powell, *The First Nine Books of the Danish History of Saxo Grammaticus: With Some Considerations on Saxo's Sources, Historical Methods, and Folk-Lore.*

Fisher & Davidson
Peter Fisher, trans., and Hilda Ellis Davidson, ed., *Saxo Grammaticus: The History of the Danes.*

Gollancz, *Hamlet*
Israel Gollancz, ed. and trans., *Hamlet in Iceland: Being the Icelandic Romantic Ambales Saga, with Extracts from Five Ambales Rimur*

and Other Illustrative Texts, for the Most Part Now First Printed, and an Introductory Essay.

Gollancz, *Sources*
Israel Gollancz, *The Sources of Hamlet, with an Essay on the Legend.*

Herrmann
Paul Herrmann, *Erläuterungen zu den ersten neun Büchern der Dänischen Geschichte des Saxo Grammaticus.*

Olrik
Axel Olrik, *Kilderne til Sakses oldhistorie: en literaturhistorisk undersøgelse.*

Olrik and Ræder
Jørgen Olrik and Hans Ræder, eds., *Saxonis Gesta Danorum.*

PMLA
Publications of the Modern Language Association.

Saxostudier
Ivan Boserup, ed., *Saxostudier (Saxo-kollokvierne ved Københavns Universitet).*

TAPA
Transactions of the American Philological Association.

ZfdA
Zeitschrift für deutsches Altertum und deutsche Litteratur.

Notes

Introduction

Part One

1. For a succinct survey of Saxo's life and work, with bibliography, see Inge Skovgaard-Petersen's article, "Saxo," in the *Kulturhistorisk leksikon for nordisk middelalder* (Copenhagen: Rosenkilde & Bagger, 1970), 15:49–57. In German see the survey of Herrmann 2:1–42. In English see Elton & Powell, pp.ix–xxii. The articles and discussions in *Saxostudier* are a stimulating sampling of recent thinking on all aspects of Saxo's work. See also Anker Teilgård Laugesen, *Introduktion til Saxo* (Copenhagen: Gyldendal, 1972).

2. The section numbers refer to the ten sections of the translation and of the commentary. They are my divisions, not Saxo's, and are employed here and hereafter for ease of reference. Sections 1–10 correspond to *Gesta Danorum* 3.6.1–4.2.2, or Olrik & Ræder, 1:76–92. More exactly, section 1 = pp.76–77; 2 = p.77; 3 = pp.77–78; 4 = pp.78–80; 5 = pp.80–81; 6 = pp.81–83; 7 = pp.83–84; 8 = pp.85–87; 9 = pp.87–91; 10 = pp.91–92.

3. See in general, Olrik, vols. 1–2; Herrmann, vol. 2; and Kurt Schier, *Sagaliteratur* (Stuttgart: J. B. Metzler, 1970),

pp.72–91. On the relationship of the *fornaldarsögur* to oral storytelling, see Peter Buchholz, *Vorzeitkunde: Mündliches Erzählen und Überliefern im mittelalterlichen Skandinavien nach dem Zeugnis von Fornaldarsaga und eddischer Dichtung*, Skandinavistische Studien 13 (Neumünster, 1980).

4. Olrik, 1:18–22. On the dispute concerning Saxo's sources, see Hermann Schneider, *Nordgermanische Heldensage*, pp.230–31, 249.

We do not know the extent to which the twelfth-century and thirteenth-century Danes accepted or rejected the traditional biography of Hamlet as a historical account. Saxo and all the other early Danish writers who mention Hamlet (see Appendix I) present him to their readers as a historical figure, though they do not agree on the details. But modern studies of contemporary legends reveal that attitudes in the same community concerning the same legend can range from belief to scorn: see Linda Dégh and Andrew Vázsonyi, "Legend and Belief," *Genre* 4 (1971): 281–304. It is not hard to imagine that some Danes believed Hamlet to have been historical, while doubting various details of the tradition; and others may have been complete skeptics. But the doubters, if doubters there were, have left us no record.

5. However, for all we know about the distribution of the legend in Denmark, which is very little, the tradition may have been well known only in Jutland. Moreover, it is not likely that even all Jutes knew and told the story. For in the case of a related genre, the *Zaubermärchen* (that is, the fairy tale, or, more precisely, Aarne-Thompson, Types 300–749, and similar tales), Bengt Holbek has recently shown that in late nineteenth-century Jutland, most of the active bearers of this genre were men (about 70 percent), whereas most of the ballad-singers were women, so that the former could be characterized as a predominantly male genre and the latter as a predominantly female genre, at least in nineteenth-century Jutland. In addition, Holbek found a marked correlation between the repertoire of male and female storytellers and the sex of the principal character in the fairy tales: men preferred male heroes (and most fairy tales have

male heroes), whereas women preferred heroines. Finally, Holbek discovered that the narrators of *Zaubermärchen* were almost exclusively members of the rural proletariat ("Eine neue Methode zur Interpretation von Zaubermärchen," *Jahrbuch für Volkskunde und Kulturgeschichte* 23 [1980]: 74–79).

The Hamlet legend, with its male hero and its male adversaries and its interest in revenge and rule, was probably a story told mostly by men to men rather than by or to women or children. If so, by which men? In *Hamlet: til forklaring af Hamletskikkelsen* (Copenhagen: Gyldendal, 1924), Johannes V. Jensen saw the legend as a fantasy tale of the humblest folk, the thralls, in which case it functioned like a *Zaubermärchen*. But the Hamlet legend is not the story of a poor lad who weds a princess but rather of a king's and queen's son who weds a girl of like rank. The thralls, like their nineteenth-century successors in rural Jutland, probably told the familiar *Zaubermärchen*, while the Hamlet story gave expression to the fantasies of a more privileged class of men.

6. Richard Cleasby and Gudbrand Vigfusson, *An Icelandic-English Dictionary,* 2d ed. (Oxford: Oxford University Press, Clarendon Press, 1957), s.v. "amlóði"; Ivar Aasen, *Norsk ordbog*, 4th ed. (Kristiania: A. Cammermeyer, 1918), s.v. "Amlod."

7. *Erikskrönikan*, ed. Rolf Pipping (Uppsala: Almqvist & Wiskells Boktr. AB, 1963), vv.3914–17.

8. For occurrences of the word or name outside Scandinavia, see Gollancz, *Sources*, pp.49–61; and Frederic Amory, "The Medieval Hamlet: A Lesson in the Use and Abuse of Myth," *Deutsche Vierteljahrsschrift für Literaturwissenschaft und Geistesgeschichte* 51 (1977): 374–79.

On the etymology, see Carl Säve, "Om Hamlets namn och betydelsen deraf," *Nordisk universitets tidsskrift* 10 (1866): 87–102; Detter, pp.1–25; Kemp Malone, "On the Etymology of Hamlet," *Philological Quarterly* 4 (1925): 158–60; "Etymologies for Hamlet," *Review of English Studies* 3 (1927): 257–71; "More Etymologies for Hamlet," *Review of English Studies* 4 (1928): 257–69; "Hamlet and Oskeladd," *Scandinavian Studies and*

Notes 10 (1928/29): 138–41; E. Bergdal, "Hamlet's Name," *Scandinavian Studies and Notes* 10 (1928/29): 159–75; "The Hamlet Yrya," *Scandinavian Studies and Notes* 11 (1930/31): 79–89; Gollancz, *Sources*, pp.49–61, 315–16; A. Nordfelt, "Om det äldre Hamletproblemet: namnet och typen," in *Språkvetenskapliga sällskapets i Uppsala förhandlingar, 1925–1927* (Uppsala, 1927), 2:55–94: R. Meissner, "Der Name Hamlet," *Indogermanische Forschungen* 45 (1927): 370–94; Jan de Vries, *Altnordisches etymologisches Wörterbuch* (Leiden: E. J. Brill, 1961), s.v. "Amlóði"; and Wolfgang Krause, "Die Hamletstrophe Snæbjǫrns," in *Festschrift für Konstantin Reichardt*, ed. Christian Gellinek, pp.93–94. Several investigators (Meissner, de Vries, Krause) connect *Amlóði* with Old Icelandic *amla* 'toil', which derives in turn from *ama* 'molest, bother.'

9. Elton & Powell, pp.408–09; Olrik, 2:158; Otto L. Jiriczek, "Die Amlethsage auf Island," *Germanistische Abhandlungen* 12 (1896): 71 n.1; Schneider, *Nordgermanische Heldensage*, p.243.

10. For the name *Hamlet*, see E. G. Withycombe, comp., *The Oxford Dictionary of English Christian Names* (Oxford: Oxford University Press, Clarendon Press, 1945), s.v. "Hamo(n)." He derives it from Old German *Haimo*, from *haimi* 'house, home.' According to Withycombe, the name was introduced into England by the Normans. *Hamlet* and *Hamnet* survived as names into the eighteenth-century.

Although Shakespeare's own short-lived son was named Hamnet, it was presumably not Shakespeare who renamed Amleth, since the name *Hamlet* was used already in the *Ur-Hamlet.*

11. *Series dynastarum et regum Daniae* 3. 7. The Latin text is quoted in Gollancz, *Hamlet*, pp. lxii–lxiii. The saga hero is a Spaniard only in the sense that his grandfather Donrik ruled over Spain, Hispania, and Cimbria. He himself is born in Cimbria, east of northern France, that is, the Cimbric Chersonese, most of which is Danish.

12. Accessible sources for the saga are Jiriczek, "Die Amlethsage," pp.59–108, who compares three seventeenth-century

manuscripts, and Gollancz, *Hamlet*, who give the text, without normalization, of a single late manuscript together with an English version. In my own summary of this complex narrative, much is necessarily omitted. On the genre, see Margaret Schlauch, *Romance in Iceland* (Princeton, N.J.: Princeton University Press, 1934).

The remark of Fisher & Davidson, 1:67, that the *Ambales Saga* was told by old women in seventeenth-century Iceland, seems to confuse the anonymous composer of this saga with the "wretched old men and women and persons of that sort" ("vetulis anibusque et ejusdem furfuris homuncionibus") from whom Torfæus recalled hearing the tale of Amloði.

13. It is nowhere explained how Ambales is able to forsee that a great storm is on the way and that its force would stop the water in its path and drive it back up again.

14. In Ambales' poem the word here rendered as "stuck" (*stunginn*) can mean "stabbed" or "hidden" (Jiriczek, "Die Amlethsage," p.84). "Cart" is, of course, used metaphorically for bed. Thus he says he saw a man hidden/stabbed under a cart/bed.

15. Or, as we should say, the evening of the seventh day, New Year's Eve.

16. Jón Árnason, *Íslenskar pjodsögur og æfintýri* (Leipzig: J. C. Hinrichs, 1864), 2:505–8. See also Einar Sveinsson, *Verzeichnis Isländischer Märchenvarianten,* FF Communications, No. 83 (Helsinki: Academia Scientiarum Fennica, 1929), Type 1696. For the sake of brevity I have summarized only the beginning and the end of Hildur's tale. On the French folktale "La Reine Châtiée," which has occasionally been put forth as a parallel to Saxo's story (Max Lüthi, "Hamlet in der Gascogne," *Shakespeare-Jahrbuch* 87/88 [1952]: 48–57), see Alexander Krappe, "Shakespeare in Romance Folklore," *Neuphilologische Mitteilungen* 27 (1926): 65–76, who shows that the tale probably entered oral tradition from French performances of Shakespeare's *Hamlet.*

17. Konrad Maurer, *Isländische Volkssagen der Gegenwart* (Leipzig: J. C. Hinrichs, 1860), pp.287–90, reports hearing the tale in Iceland in 1858.

Part Two

1. On Telemachos, see Eduard Fuchs, "Die Entstehung der Hamletsage," *Ernte* 9 (June 1928): 26–27; and P. Th. Justesen, "Telemach und *Hamlet*," *Wiener Blätter für die Freunde der Antike* 6 (1929): 75–76.

On Orestes, see Gilbert Murray, *Hamlet and Orestes: A Study in Traditional Types;* Florence M. Anderson, "The Insanity of the Hero – An Intrinsic Detail of the Orestes Vendetta," *TAPA* 58 (1927): 43–62; and C. W. Eckert, "The Festival Structure of the Orestes-Hamlet Tradition," *Comparative Literature* 15 (1963): 321–37.

On Havelok the Dane, see Gollancz, *Sources*, pp.37–61.

Other heroes have also been likened to Hamlet:

Kullervo: E. N. Setälä, "Kullervo-Hamlet: Ein sagenvergleichender Versuch," *Finnisch-Ugrische Forschungen* 3 (1903): 61–97; 7 (1907): 188–264; 10 (1910): 44–127; and Kaarle Krohn, *Kalevalastudien*, FF Communications, no.76 (Helsinki: Academia Scientiarum Fennica, 1928), pp.29–30.

Boeve de Hamtone: Rudolf Zenker, *Boeve-Amlethus: Das altfranzösische Epos von Boeve de Hamtone und der Ursprung der Hamletsage.*

Ambrosius: Niels Lukman, "British and Danish Traditions," *Classica et Mediaevalia* 6 (1944): 88–99.

Kai Khusrau: Otto L. Jiriczek, "Hamlet in Iran," *Zeitschrift des Vereins für Volkskunde* 10 (1900): 353–64; Heinrich Lessman, *Die Kyrossage in Europa* (Charlottenburg: A. Gertz, 1906). Several of these comparisons are criticized by Herrmann, 2:271–83.

For other comparisons, see R. G. Latham, *Two Dissertations on the Hamlet of Saxo Grammaticus and of Shakespear* (London: Williams & Norgate, 1872); Adolf Zinzow, *Die Hamletsage an und mit verwandten Sagen erläutert* (Halle: Buchhandlung des Waisenhauses, 1877); Kemp Malone, *The Literary History of Hamlet,* Anglistische Forschungen, no.59

(Heidelberg: Carl Winter, 1923); and Franz Rolf Schröder, "Der Ursprung der Hamletsage," *Germanisch-Romanische Monatschrift* 26 (1938): 81–108.

2. On recurrent features in hero legends, see, for example, Archer Taylor, "The Biographical Pattern in Traditional Narrative," *Journal of the Folklore Institute* 1 (1964): 114–29.

3. These and other sources for the legend can be conveniently consulted in Paul Herrmann, *Die Geschichte von Hrolf Kraki, aus dem Isländischen übersetzt, erläutert und mit saggeschichtlichen Parallelen versehen* (Torgau: F. Jacobs Buchhandlung, 1905), and in G. N. Garmonsway, Jacqueline Simpson, and Hilda Ellis Davidson, *Beowulf and Its Analogues* (New York: E. P. Dutton & Co., Dutton Paperback, 1971), especially pp.124–41.

4. It is not clear whether the slain queen is Signe, mother of Harald and Halfdan, or Ulfhild, Froði's original wife.

5. Regin addresses Froði's men from outside the hall, with a message for the king. Since Regin owes no allegiance to the king's men and has no desire to warn them of anything, he does not construct the message in such a way as to make its import obvious. Presumably he would not be greatly disappointed if the king also should miss its point, but that does not happen. In the first half of the poem he says that Regin and the sons and/or partisans of the former king are outside, and bids this be told to Froði. But the drunken men inside the hall mistake the name *Regin* (that is, *Reginn*) for the common noun "rain" (*regn*) and comment that it is no great news if there is rain outside.

The second half of the poem restates, or elaborates on, the first part. Here Regin plays upon the name *Var* (*Varr*) and the adjective *wary (varr)* and also the expression "to drive a nail of precaution" (*slá varnagla,* that is, drive a *var*-nail), which means metaphorically "to take precautions, give a warning." Thus, in the last clause Regin says that (= a wary man = Regin) drove a nail of precaution for (= has given a warning to) Var (= another wary man = Froði). The two preceding clauses—Var forged nails, and Var put heads on them—are certainly intended to bear both a literal and a figurative meaning, but the metaphors allow of more than one interpretation, so that it is unclear whether the two wary ones are Hroar, Helgi, Regin or Froði. If the metaphors refer to the plotting of Hroar and Helgi, the last clause could conceivably have three different meanings: Var drove for Var a nail of precaution (so the king's men understand it); Regin has assured the success of the plot (the way Regin may mean it); Regin has now warned Froði (the way Froði takes it). See Detter, pp.10–11; Herrmann, *Die Geschichte von Hrolf Kraki*, pp.127–28 n.11; and Richard Cleasby and Gubrand Vigfusson, *An Icelandic-English Dictionary*, 2d ed. (Oxford: Oxford University Press, Clarendon Press, 1957), s.v. "varnagli."

6. The earth house (*jarðhús*) seems to be a room or passageway near the hall through which a man might escape or in which he might seek concealment during hostilities, as Hroar and Helgi do on Vifil's island earlier. It is presumably the same as that which Saxo describes as the dark and narrow tunnels wherein Frodi perishes. Tacitus (*Germania* 16) mentions underground caves in which folk stored their produce and also took refuge during very cold weather.

7. Sigrið's choosing to perish with Froði implies that they are wed (Detter, pp.9–10). So in chapter 10 of the lost *Skjöldunga saga* (approximately contemporary with Saxo), known in the Latin abstract made by Arngrímur Jónsson at the end of the sixteenth century, it is said that Ingjald (= Froði) slew his half-brother Halfdan, became the king of Denmark, and wed the widowed Sigrið. Notice also *Völsunga saga*, chapter 8, where Signy prefers to remain in the burning hall with her husband.

8. On the kinds of change which may occur in oral stories in the course of transmission, see Stith Thompson, *The Folktale* (New York: Holt, Rinehart & Winston, 1946), pp.435–37; and Joseph Fortenrose, *Python: A Study of Delphic Myth and Its Origins* (Berkeley and Los Angeles: University of California Press, 1959), pp.5–8.

9. Aarne-Thompson, Type 502. An accessible text of this tale is Grimm no. 136, "Der Eisenhans." If we compare it with the saga episode, we see that Regin and Vifil correspond to the folktale's wild man, with whom the hero dwells for a time; the jarl's estate corresponds to the king's palace, to which the hero comes in disguise; the hood corresponds to the hat that the hero always wears; Signy's recognition of Hroar when his hood falls off corresponds to the princess's seeing the hero's golden hair when he once removes his cap; the horse ridden backwards corresponds to the hero's lame horse; Froði's banquet corresponds to the folktale monarch's festival, which is a ruse to attract the hero; and, finally, the recognition of Ham and Hrani as king's sons corresponds to the recognition of the gardener youth as a prince. As often when two oral tales combine, the one is not simply added to the other but commingles with it.

10. Axel Olrik, *Danmarks heltedigtning,* 1:175–79; Andreas Heusler, "Zur Skiöldungendichtung," *ZfdA* 48 (1906): 76–78; Gustav Neckel, "Studien über Fróði," *ZfdA* 48 (1906): 161; Oscar Olson, "The Relation of the *Hrólfs Saga Kraka* and the *Bjarkarímur* to *Beowulf,*" *Scandinavian Studies* 3 (1916): 67; Herrmann, 2:271–72; H. Schneider, *Nordgermanische Heldensage*, p.237.

11. For an investigation of the causes of narrative inconsistencies in Homeric oral poetry, see my monograph, *The Conference Sequence: Patterned Narration and Narrative Inconsistency in the Odyssey*, University of California Publications in Classical Studies, vol.8 (Berkeley and Los Angeles, 1972).

12. Detter, pp.7–18.

13. Elton & Powell, pp.402–03. Fontenrose, *Python,* pp.5–6, makes a useful distinction between the terms "version" and "variant." The former refers to different forms of a story that employ approximately the same characters and places. Different tellings of the Hamlet story are therefore different versions of the story. When an oral story has traveled to a new locality and acquired new names for its characters and places, a new variant comes into being. Thus the legends of Hamlet and of H and H are

variants of the same story. Notice that these terms do not imply the existence of a correct form of the story from which these forms vary; rather, all forms of a story are versions or variants or both, as the case may be.

14. Livy does not mention the killing of Brutus's father; he does mention the killing of the brother, though he does not explain the king's motives for killing each of them (*Histories* 4. 68. 2). The murder of Brutus's father for his wealth is implied by Diodorus Siculus (*Library of History* 10. 20. 22) and is mentioned by Dio Cassius (*Roman History* 2, frag. 11. 10 [ed. Boissevain]). Valerius Maximus (*Memorable Sayings and Deeds* 7.2) mentions the brother and gives the cause as his "keen mind."

15. Different sources give different reasons for the visit to the oracle. Cicero (*De divinatione* 1. 22, citing Accius's play *Brutus*) details a foreboding dream Tarquinius had that foretold the loss of his throne; Dio Cassius (*Roman History* 2, in Zonaras *Epitome of History* 7.11.9) mentions two omens that indicated the eventual expulsion of the Tarquins. So one or another divine foreboding of the expulsion of the king generally furnishes the occasion for the inquiry at the oracle. But according to Valerius Maximus (*Memorable Sayings and Deeds* 7. 2), Tarquinius simply sent his sons to Delphi to do honor to the god.

16. Other sources also explain Brutus's gold-filled stick in one or both of these ways. Zonaras agrees with Livy (*Histories* 1. 56. 9–10) that the stick is a symbol of its bearer. He says (*Epitome of History* 7. 11. 12) it depicted the role Brutus was playing, for Brutus had secretly hollowed it out and poured gold into it, indicating through it how behind his folly there likewise lay concealed an intelligent mind. Thus the stick is a secret message to Apollo explaining Brutus's apparent and actual selves. Other writers agree with Dionysios (*Roman Antiquities* 4. 69. 3) that it is a secret and valuable votive offering, necessarily disguised since it was unsafe for Brutus to venerate the deity openly: Valerius Maximus (*Memorable Sayings and Deeds* 7. 2); Dio Cassius (*Roman History* 2, frag. 11. 10 [ed. Boissevain]); Zonaras (*Epitome of History* 7. 11. 12).

17. The ancient writers have little to say about the official mission of Titus and Arruns to Delphi, though according to Dio Cassius (*Roman History* 2 in Zonaras *Epitome of History* 7. 11. 10) Apollo answered their inquiry with the response that Tarquinius would be driven from his rule when a dog should employ human speech, which Tarquinius was confident would never happen. On the oracles, see Joseph Fontenrose, *The Delphic Oracle* (Berkeley and Los Angeles: University of California Press, 1978), p.314 (Q138–39).

The unconnected quality of this episode is somewhat reduced if one assumes that Brutus's gold-filled stick pleases the god as an offering as well as informs him metaphorically (gold-filled stick = Brutus) of Brutus's hidden quality of mind, so that Apollo in turn repays Brutus by revealing metaphorically (mother = earth), that is, in a fashion that only a clever mind can apprehend, the precondition that Rome's next ruler must satisfy.

18. I follow Livy's account of the Lucretia episode. Dionysios tells it somewhat differently (there is, for example, no contest of wives). The tale is discussed in detail by Photeine P. Bourboulis, *Studies in the History of Modern Greek Story-Motives,* Hellenika, suppl. 2 (Thessalonica, 1953), pp.53–103. Lucretia's husband, L. Tarquinius Collatinus, belongs to the same generation as Brutus and the king's sons Arruns, Titus, and Sextus, and is related to the royal house, as his name indicates. His grandfather, Arruns Tarquinius, is the brother of Tarquinius Priscus, father of Tarquinius Superbus.

19. According to Dio Cassius (*Roman History* 2, frag. 11. 12 [ed. Boissevain]), Brutus's companions mock him not only for his gift but also when he pretends to fall in order to kiss the earth.

20. In the legend of Virginia (for example, Livy *Histories* 3. 44–54), (i) the lustful Decemvir Appius Claudius tries to get access to the pretty and modest maiden Virginia; (ii) her father kills her to prevent her from falling into Appius's hands; (iii) the angry plebs secedes to the Sacred Mount, (iv) and thereby forces the Decemviri to abdicate. See further, Ettore Pais, *Ancient Legends of Roman History*, trans. Mario Cosenza (London: Swan Sonnenschein &

Co., 1906), pp.185–203. In a third variant of the story (Livy 8. 28), (i) the creditor L. Papirius tries to seduce the young, handsome youth C. Publilius, who is in debt on behalf of his father; (ii) spurned, Lucius has the boy beaten; (iii) a multitude of angry folk gathers at the Senate House; (iv) as a consequence the practice of imprisoning debtors is outlawed. The legend type is also found in Greek tradition. In the story of Archias and the youth Aktaion (Diodorus Siculus *Library of History* 8. 10; Pseudo-Plutarch *Moralia* 772e–773b; Maximus of Tyre *Lectures* 18. 1; scholia on Apollonios *Argonautika* 4. 1212), (i) Archias, a member of the Bakchiad family that rules Corinth, is unable to persuade Aktaion to return his love; (ii) Archias attempts to abduct the youth, who literally is torn apart in the ensuing struggle; (iii) Aktaion's father places the boy's body in the agora and curses the Bakchiads, (iv) whom the Corinthians eventually expel. On the Greek story, see further Joseph Fortenrose, *Orion: The Myth of the Hunter and the Huntress,* University of California Publications in Classical Studies, vol.23 (Berkeley and Los Angeles, 1981), pp. 38–40.

21. Formally Lucretia's killing herself recalls Amleth's killing of the eavesdropper in the same scene, but functionally the killings seem to have nothing in common. Lucretia's suicide corresponds in spirit, rather, to Geruth's decision to abstain from sexual relations; that is, after the woman is reproached (by herself or by the hero) for sexual misconduct, she makes a gesture of chastity (suicide or abstention). On the other hand, the eavesdropping agent of the Danish king is somewhat reminiscent of the lustful son of the Roman king, at least to the extent that each sneaks into the woman's bedroom one night. There is archaeological evidence for an ancient tradition of a more lustful Lucretia, if Jocelyn Small is correct in her interpretation of a scene found on a group of Etruscan funerary urns of the first century B.C. See her article, "The Death of Lucretia," *American Journal of Archaeology* 80 (1976): 349–60.

22. Detter, pp.1–25; Marion Taylor, *A New Look at the Old Sources of "Hamlet,"* Studies in English Literature, vol. 42 (The Hague and Paris: Mouton, 1968); Elton & Powell, p. 410; Otto L.

Jiriczek, "Hamlet in Iran," *Zeitschrift des Vereins für Volkskunde* 10 (1900): 364.

23. Gollancz, *Sources*, pp. 27–31. A similar view is put forth by F. J. Billeskov Jansen in *Dansk litteraturhistorie*, ed. P. H. Traustedt, 2d. ed. (Copenhagen: Politiken, 1976), 1:76.

24. Aarne-Thompson, Type 961B. See further my Commentary, sec.6.

25. Gollancz, *Sources*, pp.28, 32–33.

26. Elton & Powell, p.409. Zenker, *Boeve-Amlethus*, pp.85–88, argues that the similarities of Amleth's speech to the Jutes with Brutus's address to the Romans in Dionysios (4. 77–83) is the result of Saxo's having access to an epitome of Dionysios's history, but Herrmann, 2:277, points out that similar situations produce similar topics in classical rhetoric.

27. This is the view expressed, for example, by Herrmann, 2:276–78.

28. Jiriczek, "Hamlet in Iran," p.358.

29. Consequently, we should reject the thesis of Niebuhr stated in the middle of the last century and commonly reiterated since then, that the legend of Brutus's feigned madness was spun out of the cognomen Brutus. See, for example, Schur in *Paulys Realencyclopädie der classischen Altertumswissenschaft,* suppl. 5 (Stuttgart: Alfred Druckenmüller, 1931), col. 357. The name *Brutus* did not by some unknown process call the plot of the Hero as Fool into being ex nihilo; rather, Romans attached and adapted the plot of an existing migratory legend to the name.

30. See Jiriczek, "Hamlet in Iran," pp.353–64. My summary of the story is taken mostly from *The Sháhnáma of Firdausí,* trans. Arthur George Warner and Edmond Warner (London: Kegan Paul, Trench, Trübner & Co., 1906), vol.2

Part Three

1. There seems to be no good term available in English to describe this making of a speech act into a literary text, though the practice is certainly common and probably as old as literature itself.

We could coin *literaturization*, like the Italian *letteraturizzazione*, but I fear the word would be too thick ever to flow easily from our lips or pens. On the Italian term, see George A. Kennedy, *Classical Rhetoric and Its Christian and Secular Tradition from Ancient to Modern Times* (Chapel Hill: University of North Carolina Press, 1980), pp.5, 108–19. He uses it to refer to the transference of rhetorical techniques from an oral medium in a civic context ("primary rhetoric") to a literary medium in a personal context ("secondary rhetoric").

2. There is a detailed account in Herrmann, 1:444–92, 2:29–42. See also the following articles in *Saxostudier:* Palle W. Neilsen, "Den typiske Saxo-sætning," pp.67–75; Birgit Sterll, "Til belysning af stilistiske Forskelle i *Gesta Danorum*," pp.76–78; and Gerhard Bendz, "Saxos stilistiska förebilder, metrik, och prosarytm," pp.95–103.

3. Robert H. Stein, *The Method and Message of Jesus' Teachings* (Philadelphia: Westminster Press, 1978), pp.13–14.

4. Inge Skovgaard-Petersen, "Saxo," in *Kulturhistorisk leksikon for nordisk middelalder* (Copenhagen: Rosenkilde & Bagger, 1970), 15:50. See also her article, "*Gesta Danorum*s genremæssige placering," in *Saxostudier*, pp.20–29. The question of whether Saxo was acquainted with Geoffrey of Monmouth's *Historia regum Britanniae* is discussed by Niels Lukman, "Saxos kendskab til Galfred af Monmouth," *Dansk historisk tidsskrift* 10 (1942–44).

5. On this point see, in general, Franz Blatt's introduction, in Olrik & Ræder, 2:x–xiii (= pp. xxi–xxv), and his article, "Saxo, en repræsentant for det tolvte århundredes renæssance," in *Saxo-studier*, pp.11–19.

6. Karsten Friis-Jensen, *Saxo og Vergil: en analyse af 1931-udgavens Vergilparalleler*, Opuscula Graecolatina, no.1 (Copenhagen: Museum Tusculanum, 1975), p.10. Although Friis-Jensen's investigation of over fifty alleged borrowings of Saxo from Vergil, of which Friis-Jensen eventually acknowledges only fourteen, throws considerable doubt on the correctness of the absolute

figures, there is no doubt that Valerius was Saxo's most important stylistic model.

7. On the pointed style, see Walter C. Summers, ed., *Select Letters of Seneca* (London: Macmillan & Co., 1910), pp.xv–xli.

8. The *Compendium Saxonis* forms the first part of the *Jutish Chronicle*. For the text of the *Chronica Jutensis*, see *Scriptores minores historiae Danicae medii aevi*, ed. M. Cl. Gertz (Copenhagen: G. E. C. Gad, 1917), 1:197–439; the account of "Ambletus" appears on pp.246–55. It is also printed in Gollancz, *Hamlet*, pp.260–72.

9. In so generalizing, I do not assert that Saxo never allowed his Latin models in any way to influence the content of his narrative, since the contrary is plainly true. For an example, see Herrmann, 2:33–35; on the question of the extent of Saxo's borrowing, see Bendz, "Saxos förebilder," pp.95–96, and Jørgen Raasted, "Saxos benyttelse af Justin-handskriftet *Gl. kgl. Saml.* 450 fol.," p.104, in *Saxostudier*. I do, however, claim that this influence on content is sporadic and exceptional and extends rarely, if ever, to form. My notion of form here is similiar to what Walter Burkert has recently called the "crystallization of a tale." See his *Structure and History in Greek Mythology and Ritual* (Berkeley and Los Angeles: University of California Press, 1979), especially pp.18–22.

10. See, in general, the discussions of Axel Olrik, "Epische Gesetze der Volksdichtung," *ZfdA* 51 (1909): 1–12; Hermann Gunkel, *Genesis,* 7th. ed. (Göttingen: Vandenhoeck & Ruprecht, 1966), pp. xxvii–lvi; and Max Lüthi, *Das Europäische Volksmärchen: Form und Wesen*, 2d. ed. (Bern: A. Francke, 1960). On Olrik's celebrated "epic laws," see further, Laurits Bødker, *Folk Literature (Germanic)* (Copenhagen: Rosenkilde & Bagger, 1965), s.v. "Episk lov." (An English translation of Olrik's article appears in Alan Dundes, *The Study of Folklore* [Englewood Cliffs, N.J.: Prentice-Hall, 1965], pp.129–41, and the pertinent portion of Gunkel's book is available in English as *The Legends of Genesis,* trans. W. H.

Carruth [New York: Schocken Books, Schocken Paperback, 1964], pp.37–87.) Carl Lindahl, "On the Borders of Oral and Written Art," *Folklore Forum* 11 (1978): 94–123, gives a salutary caution against exaggerating the difference between oral and written narrative.

11. Gunkel, *Genesis*, p. xxxvi.

12. Olrik, "Epische Gesetze," p.8; Gunkel, *Genesis*, pp. xxxix–xlv; Vladimir Propp, *The Morphology of the Folktale*, 2d. ed. (Austin and London: University of Texas Press, 1968), pp.75–78.

13. Olrik, "Epische Gesetze," p.5; Gunkel, *Genesis*, p. xxxvi; William A. Lessa, "'Discoverer-of-the-Sun': Mythology as a Reflection of Culture," in *The Anthropologist Looks at Myth*, comp. Melville Jacobs, ed. John Greenway (Austin and London: University of Texas Press, 1966), pp.34–35.

14. Cf. Gunkel, *Genesis*, p. xxxv.

15. Olrik, "Epische Gesetze," p.5.

16. In the *Vita Amlethi* there is one bare exception to the rule of two. Following the scene of the sexual test in the woods, the participants return to the hall, where the bystanders question them in turn (sec.4). They interrogate first Amleth, then the girl, and finally the housecarls who had been Amleth's escorts. Thus four characters appear to be present—Amleth, the girl, the housecarls, and the interrogating bystanders—but so far only two interact at a time. Then one of the housecarls, Amleth's foster brother, steps forward to speak on his own. At this point, then, Amleth and his foster brother are active: the latter speaks, and the former replies. The girl is forgotten. What of the bystanders and the other housecarls? They become an active audience to the conversation, for Amleth's words rouse them to laughter. Instead of retiring into inactivity, they remain mildly engaged in the interaction.

17. The number three, so common in European folktales, plays a minor role. Tripartition is prominent only in episodes that the legend has borrowed from folktale (Commentary, sec.6). Thus the king of Britain has three visitors (Amleth and his escorts), Amleth censures three foods (bread, meat, and drink), and he finds three faults in the queen's behavior. On the prominence of the number

three in European folktales, see, for example, Olrik, "Epische Gesetze," pp. 4–5, and on three as a pattern number more generally, see Alan Dundes, *Every Man His Way* (Englewood Cliffs, N.J.: Prentice-Hall, 1968), pp.401–24.

18. The point is often made, though discussions are few. But see C. M. Bowra, *Heroic Poetry* (London: Macmillan, 1952), pp.302–6.

19. Ibid., pp.302–4; cf. Gunkel, *Genesis*, p. xxxvi.

20. So also in Homer's *Odessey* (13. 361–71) the poet relates how Odysseus and Athene conceal the hero's treasure in a cave, but never mentions it again.

21. Olrik, 2:157, 181, emphasizes the similarity of the present story and of the Danish ballad in the treatment of nature. The ballad as genre appears to have reached Denmark before 1200.

On landscape, see Peter Hallberg, *The Icelandic Saga*, trans. Paul Schach (Lincoln: University of Nebraska Press, 1962), p.71 and notes. Cf. also Gunkel, *Genesis*, p. xliv; for similar remarks about Hebrew legend.

22. Of course, Saxo's narrative is not unique in mixing the heroic and the romantic, for the mixture is frequently found in the *fornaldarsögur* and in other literature. See Margaret Schlauch, *Romance in Iceland* (Princeton, N.J.: Princeton University Press, 1934), and W. P. Ker, *Epic and Romance: Essays on Medieval Literature*, 2d. ed. (1908; reprint ed., New York: Dover Publications, 1957), pp.53–57.

23. Ben E. Perry, "The Ancient Greek Capacity for Viewing Things Separately," *TAPA* 68 (1937): 403–27. See further, James A. Notopoulos, "Parataxis in Homer," *TAPA* 80 (1949): 1–23; and Lüthi, "Volksmärchen," pp.37–62.

24. Gunkel, *Genesis*, p. xxxvii.

25. Ibid., pp. xxxviii–xxxix.

26. Ibid., p. xxxix.

27. See note 2, above.

28. Cf. Olrik, "Epische Gesetze," pp.6–7.

29. Ibid., p.10.

30. Ibid., p.8.

31. Cf. Bowra, *Heroic Poetry,* pp.313–14.

32. Thaddaeus Zielinski, "Die Behandlung gleichzeitiger Ereignisse im antiken Epos," *Philologus,* suppl. 8 (1899–1901): 412 (that is, *die gleichzeitige analysirend-desultorische Methode*). See further, Hans-Hugo Steinhoff, *Die Darstellung gleichzeitiger Geschenisse im mittelhochdeutschen Epos, Medium Aevum* 4 (Munich, 1964); and Tilman Krischer, *Formale Koventionen der homerischen Epik, Zetemata* 56 (Munich, 1971), pp.91–129.

33. Olrik, 1:93–94. On the name, see Gunnar Knudsen, Marius Kristensen, and Rikard Hornby, *Danmarks gamle personnavne* (Copenhagen: G. E. C. Gad, 1936–48), vol.1, s.v. "Hermuthrud."

34. Inger M. Boberg, *Dansk folketradition* (Copenhagen: Munksgaard, 1962), p.81. See also Bengt Holbek, "Oppositions and Contrasts in Folklore," in *Proceedings of the Folklore Society of London: Folklore Studies in the Twentieth Century,* ed. Venetia Newall (London: Boydell & Brewer, 1980), pp.236–39.

35. Fengi's friend is one of a number of characters of some importance in the *Vita Amlethi* who are unnamed. Others are Amleth's foster siblings, his two escorts on the voyage to Britain, the king of Britain, and Amleth's first wife. Medieval Danish stories have a smaller cast of characters, of whom fewer are named, than, for example, Icelandic stories have (Olrik, 1:18–20). So the nameless condition of Fengi's friend is probably a consequence of Danish oral storytelling style in general, which Saxo reflects.

Part Four

1. Basel, 1534, and Frankfurt, 1576. There is a list of editions and translations of Saxo in Olrik & Ræder, 1:555–61.

2. The publishing history is given in Frank S. Hook, *The French Bandello,* University of Missouri Studies 22, no.1 (Columbia, 1948), p.49. Of the first edition (Paris, 1570) and several other reported editions, no copies are known to exist. The comment of Fisher & Davidson, 1:67, that "the original French work . . . was being written from 1560 onwards," is misleading in this connection.

3. See F. W. Schulze, "François Belleforest's *Histoire tragique d'Amleth,*" in *Im Dienste der Sprache: Festschrift für Victor Klemperer,* ed. Horst Heintze and Erwin Silzer, pp.362–74, and a series of articles by Arthur P. Stabler: "King Hamlet's Ghost in Belleforest?" *PMLA* 77 (1962): 18–20; "Elective Monarchy in the Sources of *Hamlet,*" *Studies in Philology* 62 (1965): 654–61; "Melancholy, Ambition, and Revenge in Belleforest's Hamlet," *PMLA* 81 (1966): 207–13; and "The Source of the German Hamlet," *Shakespeare Studies* 5 (1969): 97–105.

4. A survey of the evidence concerning the *Ur-Hamlet* and Shakespeare's reworking of it is found in Geoffrey Bullough, *Narrative and Dramatic Sources of Shakespeare*, 7:3–59. See also E. A. J. Honigman, "The Date of *Hamlet,*" *Shakespeare Survey* 9 (1956): 24–34.

5. On English familiarity with Saxo's book, see Ethel Seaton, *Literary Relations of England and Scandinavia in the Seventeenth Century* (Oxford: Oxford University Press, Clarendon Press, 1935). Arthur P. Stabler, in "The Sources of *Hamlet*: Some Corrections of the Record," *Research Studies* 32 (1964): 207–16, finds no "evidence of an independent line of derivation from Saxo." Yngve B. Olsson, in his "In Search of Yorick's Skull: Notes on the Background of Hamlet," *Shakespeare Studies* 4 (1968): 183–220, puts forth the German humanist historian Albert Krantz as a possible intermediary source. Krantz retold Saxo's tale (which he probably got from the *Compendium Saxonis* rather than from Saxo directly) in his *Chronicles of the Northern Kingdoms: Denmark, Sweden, Norway,* which was published both in German translation (in 1546) and in the original Latin (in 1548). But in "More on the Search for Yorick's Skull; or, the Goths Refuted," *Shakespeare Studies* 7 (1974): 203–8, Stabler shows that it is not necessary to suppose Krantz had any influence on the Elizabethan *Hamlet*. The case for Krantz and especially for Saxo has been revived by Dollerup, pp.15–47, who however appears to be unaware of Stabler's work; and Fisher & Davidson, 1:67, in turn follow Dollerup.

6. Belleforest says that before Fengon murdered his brother, Fengon and Geruthe had had sexual relations; that is, Belleforest

extends the "incestuous" relationship of the brother and the widow that in Saxo's tale follows the murder, into an "incestuous adultery" that precedes it. Always the moralist, Belleforest, who has himself invented the adultery of Fengon and Geruthe, proceeds then to rail at them all the more for their wickedness. For the text, see Gollancz, *Sources*, pp.186–88. The queen's infidelity before her husband's death seems to be referred to in the play (1. 5. 42–46; 5. 2. 64). See further, J. Dover Wilson, *What Happens in Hamlet* (Cambridge: the University Press, 1935), pp.292–94.

7. On Shakespeare's reworking of his sources for *Hamlet*, I am much indebted to Robert Adger Law's study, "Belleforest, Shakespeare, and Kyd," in *Joseph Quincy Adams Memorial Studies*, ed. James G. MacManaway, Giles E. Dawson, and Edwin E. Willoughby, pp.279–94. Also useful are Ernest Jones, *Hamlet and Oedipus*, pp.173–79; Kenneth Muir, *Shakespeare's Sources*, 1:110–22; Virgil K. Whitaker, *Shakespeare's Use of Learning*, pp.251–74; and Bullough, *Narrative Sources*, especially pp.50–59. Studies on Shakespeare's use of Danish local color will be cited below.

8. Cf. the law of opening and closing in Axel Olrik, "Epische Gesetze der Volksdichtung," *ZfdA* 51 (1909): 2–3.

9. Citations from *Hamlet* are from the text of *The Riverside Shakespeare*, ed. G. Blakemore Evans (Boston: Houghton Mifflin, 1974).

10. The sheer quantity of *Hamlet* criticism gives weighty testimony to the attractive mystery of Hamlet's character. See Paul S. Conklin, *A History of "Hamlet" Criticism, 1601–1821*; Clifford Leech, "Studies in *Hamlet*: 1901–1955," *Shakespeare Survey* 9 (1956): 1–15; Stanley Wells, "A Reader's Guide to 'Hamlet,'" *Stratford-upon-Avon Studies* 5 (London, 1963): 200–207; Morris Weitz, *Hamlet and the Philosophy of Literary Criticism*; Harold Jenkins, "'Hamlet' Then till Now," *Shakespeare Survey* 18 (1965): 34–45; Laura Bohannan, "Shakespeare in the Bush," *Natural History* 75 (August–September 1966): 28–33, and often reprinted; and Paul Gottschalk, *The Meanings of Hamlet: Modes of Literary Interpretation since Bradley*.

11. It should be mentioned that statements relating Shakespeare's characters to their prototypes are often inexact, since the playwright sometimes distributes features of a source character to more than one character in his drama. Thus Horatio is generally taken to be inspired by Amleth's loyal ally, the gentlemen who was reared with him and secretly warns him of the erotic trap. But in the play his warning is entirely dropped, and the feature of his being brought up with the hero is transferred to Hamlet's friends Rosencrantz and Guildenstern (2. 2. 11).

12. Law, "Belleforest," pp.288–90; Francis Fergusson, *The Idea of a Theater* (Princeton, N.J.: Princeton University Press, 1949), pp.103–12; Whitaker, *Shakespeare's Use,* p.260. See also Richard Levin, *The Multiple Plot in English Renaissance Drama* (Chicago and London: University of Chicago Press, 1971).

13. Gunnar Sjögren, "A Contribution to the Geography of *Hamlet*," *Shakespeare Jahrbuch* 100/101 (1964/65): 273, observes that no source has yet been found for the Fortinbras subplot. Dollerup, pp.20–21, mentions the ghost, Fortinbras, and the timing of Hamlet's death as important elements of Shakespeare's play that are unknown to Saxo's and Belleforest's story.

14. For the text, see Gollancz, *Sources,* p.300.

15. Levin, *Multiple Plot*, p.23, contrasts the use of multiple plots in oral narrative and literary drama.

16. Gollancz, *Sources*, pp.180, 282.

17. Ibid., pp.236, 254.

18. The Danish background in the play has been the subject of increasing scholarly attention, from the few items mentioned by Henrik Schück, "Englische Komödianten in Skandinavien," *Skandinavisches archiv* 1 (1892): 357–86; and the survey of Laurits Pedersen, *Kronborg have* (Copenhagen: G. E. C. Gad, 1920), pp.78–84, through a series of articles published in the sixties by Gunnar Sjögren, especially "The Danish Background in Hamlet," *Shakespeare Studies* 4 (1968): 221–30, to the full-length study of Dollerup published in 1975.

19. On Elsinore, see Ingvar Andersson, "Om Hamletdramats nordiska miljö," in *Svenskt och europeiskt femtonhundratal*

(Lund: C. W. K. Gleerup, 1943), pp.129-52; Sjögren, "Danish Background," p.223; and Dollerup, pp.89-96, 144-161.

20. For a discussion, see Gösta Lagenfelt, "Danzig och Dansk: ett geografiskt och filologiskt misstag," *Finsk tidskrift* 88 (1920): 63–79; Sjögren, "Geography of *Hamlet*," pp.266–273; Dollerup, pp.110, 161–72.

21. Schück, "Englische Komödianten," pp.362–63; Dollerup, pp.127–30. Hamlet is a student at Wittenberg (1. 2. 113, 119); similarly, Horatio (1. 2. 164, 168). Hamlet refers to Rosencrantz and Guildenstern as "school-fellows" (3. 4. 202), which could refer to their preuniversity nurture (cf. 2. 2. 11); but in the First Quarto (944–45) these two are unambiguously fellow students of Hamlet's at Wittenberg.

22. The survey of the Danish names by Dollerup, pp.188–92, supersedes all previous discussions on the topic, which, except for Sjögren's, tend to be unreliable.

In the Riverside edition, Yaughan has been demoted from text to textual note.

23. This point is made by Dollerup, pp.190–91. On the Rosenkrantz family, see *Danmarks adels aarbog* 27 (Copenhagen, 1910), ed. H. R. Hiort-Lorenzen and A. Thiset, pp.370–444; and Konrad Barner and Arnold Heise, *Familien Rosenkrantz's historie,* 3 vols. (Copenhagen: C. A. Reitzel, 1874–87). On the Gyldenstjerne family, see *Danmarks adels aarbog* 43 (Copenhagen, 1926), ed. G. O. A. Von Irgens-Bergh and Louis Bobé, pp.3–37. The Gyldenstjernes died out in Denmark in 1729, but a line of the family survives in Sweden, where it is called Gyllenstierna.

24. Gunnar Sjögren, "Hamlet and the Coronation of Christian IV," *Shakespeare Quarterly* 16 (1965): 156–57; Dollerup, pp.211–12. It has been said of the Rosenkrantz family that they "are if not the oldest, most famous, and most prolific family in the Danish nobility, then at least the family that has produced proportionately the greatest number of famous and meritorious men" (cited by Ejler Haugsted, "Rosenholm," in *Danske slotte og herregårde*, 2d. ed., ed. Aage Rousell [Copenhagen: Hassing, 1967], 14:369).

25. Palle Rosenkrantz, "Rosenkrantz og Gyldenstjerne i Hamlet," *Gads danske magasin* (1909): 177–87.

26. For a survey of other Danish features in *Hamlet*, see Dollerup. On Danish drinking habits in *Hamlet*, see especially Schück, "Englische Komödianten," pp.363–65, and Dollerup, pp.122–27, 215–16. Danish fondness for drink is also mentioned several times by Saxo (2. 3. 5; 5. 14. 4; 8. 12. 1–4).

27. The passage is quoted in Troels-Lund, *Dagligt liv i norden i det sekstende århundrede,* 6th ed. (Copenhagen: Gyldendal, 1969), 3:229.

28. Fynes Moryson, *An Itinerary . . . Containing his Ten Yeeres Travell through the Twelve Dominions . . .* (1617; reprint ed., Glasgow: J. MacLehose & Sons, 1908), 4:67; John Stow, *The Annales of England* (London: G. Bishop & T. Adams, 1605), p.1436.

29. *The Works of Thomas Nashe,* ed. Ronald B. McKerrow (London: A. H. Bullen, 1904), 1:180. A. Davenport, "Shakespeare and Nashe's 'Pierce Penilesse,'" pp.371–74, and G. Blakemore Evans, "Thomas Nashe and the 'Dram of Eale,'" pp.377–78, in *Notes & Queries* 198 (1953), discuss the playwright's use of Nashe's pamphlet, some features of which can be discerned in *Hamlet*.

30. Dollerup, pp.123–24. The fact was first noticed by F. J. Furnivall in *New Shakespeare Society's Transactions* 1 (1874): 512–13. Martin Holmes, *The Guns of Elsinore* (London: Chatto & Windus, 1964), p.174, discusses Shakespeare's dramatic use of the custom.

31. Stow, *Annales*, p.1436; Dollerup, p.124.

32. Sjögren, "Danish Background," pp.221–22, and Dollerup, pp.48–60.

33. On her life, see Ethel Carleton Williams, *Anne of Denmark* (London: Longman, 1970). On Anne of Denmark and *Hamlet*, see Dollerup, pp.60–70.

34. V. C. Ravn, "'Engelske instrumentister' ved det danske hof paa Shakespeares tid," *For idé og virkelighed* 1 (1870):

75–92; Johannes Bolte, "Englische Komödianten in Dänemark und Schweden," *Shakespeare Jahrbuch* 23 (1888): 99–106; Schück, "Englische Komödianten," pp.357–86; E. K. Chambers, *The Elizabethan Stage* (Oxford: Oxford University Press, Clarendon Press, 1923), 2:270–94; Gunnar Sjögren, "Thomas Bull and Other 'English Instrumentalists' in Denmark in the 1580s," *Shakespeare Survey* 22 (1969): 119–24; Erik Wikland, *Elizabethan Players in Sweden, 1591–92* 2d. ed. (Stockholm: Almqvist & Wiksell, 1971), pp.110–63; and Dollerup, pp.173–87.

35. Ravn, "Engelske instrumentister," p.81.

36. Alf Henriques, *Shakespeare og Danmark indtil* 1840, p.15, citing Erik Pontoppidan, *Curriculum vitae* (written in Bergen in 1753, published in 1874), p.52.

37. Henriques, *Shakespeare og Danmark,* pp.43–44. Even so, the translator Johannes Boye under the influence of Saxo's narrative altered Gertrude to "Gehrud" and Fortinbras to "Kohler."

38. The following account of the Kronborg gardens and of Hamlet's grave therein is taken mostly from Laurits Pedersen's fascinating history of the garden, *Kronborg have*, pp.125–42.

39. Ibid., p.139.

40. Our own century has seen one of the happier consequences of Shakespeare's localization of the story, the open-air performances of *Hamlet* by various companies in Kronborg's large courtyard. An account of them is included in Alf Henriques's article, "Shakespeare and Denmark: 1900–1949" *Shakespeare Survey* 3 (1950): 107–15.

Commentary

1. The practice of Saxo's commentators and translators varies considerably in the rendering of proper names. The problem in simply adopting the personal names in the Latin form without the inflectional endings is that this form is sometimes quite misleading and unlike the original name. On the other hand, it is often far from clear just how one should reproduce the original name. The

forms I employ are partially re-Danicized. On Saxo's Latinization of Scandinavian names, see Marius Kristensen, "Sakses nordiske person- og stednavne," *Danske studier* 1/2 (1929): 66–73, and Kristian Hald, "Navnestoffet hos Saxo," in *Saxostudier,* pp.79–94.

2. Olrik, 2:297–298

3. *Gesta Danorum* 2. 5. 2. and 7. 1. 1.

4. On the holmgang in general, see Gwyn Jones, "Some Characteristics of the Icelandic 'Hólmganga,'" *Journal of English and Germanic Philology* 32 (1933):203–24; Marlene Ciklamini, "The Old Icelandic Duel," *Scandinavian Studies* 35 (1963):175–94; Gerd Sieg, "Die Zweikämpfe der Islandersagas," *ZfdA* 95 (1966): 1–27; and Olav Bø, "*Hólmganga* and *einvígi,*" *Mediaeval Scandinavia* 2 (1969): 132–48.

5. So Olrik, 1:58–59, 2:156–57, who suggests that linguistic change allowed a chivalric interpretation. *Leysa sik af hólmi* 'ransom oneself from the island' became, as the reflexive developed a passive sense, Old Danish *løsæs af holm*, so that (Olrik believes) the expression was understood to mean that someone else—namely, the victor—might ransom the loser after the duel. However that may be, the chivalric element certainly results in part from a changing ethos and reflects, however inconsistently, an interest in newer values and ideas. On the possibly mythological origin of the episode, see Herrmann, 2:245–48; Jan de Vries, *Altgermanische Religionsgeschichte*, 2d ed. (Berlin: Walter de Gruyter & Co., 1957), 2:137–38; and Georges Dumézil, *From Myth to Fiction*, trans. Derek Coltman (Chicago and London: University of Chicago Press, 1973), pp.193–201.

6. Petrus Erasmus Müller and Joannes Matthias Velschow, eds., *Saxonis Grammatici Historia Danica*, 1:139, followed by most interpreters.

7. The pun would be more at home in the revenge scene in Fengi's tent (sec.7). Amleth there exchanges his bound sword for his uncle's weapon, which hangs by his bed. Awakening the king, he says that Amleth is here, armed with his old crooks ("adesse Amlethum veterum uncorum suorum ope succinctum") and eager to exact the revenge he is owed for the killing of his father. While

Fengi tries in vain to draw the bound sword, Amleth cuts him down. In reality, of course, Amleth is not then armed with his old crooks, which are serving a different purpose. But there, if anywhere, one might welcome a play on "crooks" and "tricks."

8. Olrik, 2:162

9. Hermann Schneider, *Nordgermanische Heldensage*, p.228

10. *Sigrdrífumál* 35 and *Sigurðarkviða hin skamma* 12.

11. Hans Sperber, "The Conundrums in Saxo's Hamlet Episode," *PMLA* 64 (1949): 869–70.

12. If Uhland is correct in supposing that Saxo's *militare* 'fight' actually represents Icelandic *herja* 'campaign' or 'lay waste', then the double sense of Amleth's words is quite precise: In Fengi's stable there are too few horses / wolves campaigning / laying waste. See *Uhlands Schriften zur Geschichte der Dichtung und Sage* (Stuttgart, 1868), 7:205–6, cited by Herrmann, 2:254–55 n. 2.

13. Stephanus Iohannis Stephanius, ed., *Saxonis Grammatici Historiae Danicae libri XVI*, comments in his note *ad locum* that "perpaucos" is to be understood in the sense of "nimis paucos."

14. R. Meissner, "Der Name Hamlet," *Indogermanische Forschungen* 45 (1927): 389–90. *Laa* survives in the Jutish dialect, in which it means a "narrow inlet of the sea," and in the name of the island Lolland. Meissner infers that Old Danish **laar* probably refers to coastal waters since its Icelandic counterpart *lǫ́* a poetic word for "waves" or "waters," is particularly applied to the coast. The pun cannot be made in Old Icelandic, in which the corresponding words are *lær* and *lǫ́*.

15. I render "albicantis" here as an active rather than an intransitive participle, that is, "whitening, bleaching" instead of "being white," following Franz Blatt in his index verborum: Olrik & Ræder, vol.2, s.v. "albico." This is doubtless the sense that Saxo had in mind.

16. Müller & Velschow, *Historia Danica*, p.141; Detter, pp.5–6.

17. For discussions of Snæbjörn's difficult strophe, see Detter, pp.5–6; Herrmann, 2:256, 271; Gollancz, *Sources*, pp.1–8, 313–14; Wolfgang Krause, "Die Hamletstrophe Snæbjǫrns," in

Festschrift für Konstantin Reichardt, ed. Christian Gellinek, pp.87–97; and Frederic Amory, "The Medieval Hamlet," *Deutsche Vierteljahrsschrift für Literaturwissenschaft und Geistesgeschichte* 51 (1977): 357–74. The precise sense of the compound *líðmeldr 'líð*-meal', rendered here simply as "meal," is uncertain and disputed. The noun *líð* (or lið) means "host, folk, people," "ale," or "ship."

18. *Skáldskaparmál*, chap.25: "Hér er kallat hafit Amlóða kvern."

19. Cf. Meissner, "Der Name," pp.388–89 n.1; Schneider, *Heldensage,* p.229.

20. Jørgen Olrik, "'Avnebag': forklaring til en gaade i Amled-sagnet," in *Festskrift til H. F. Feilberg*, pp.98–100.

21. Sperber, "Conundrums," pp.866–68.

22. Geoffrey Bullough, *Narrative and Dramatic Sources of Shakespeare*, 7:12 n. 1.

23. Olrik, 2:160. The wordplay is not possible in Old Icelandic, as Olrik shows, since "horsehoof" is not found on Iceland, and though "cockscomb" is, it is called *Lokasjóðr* there (not *hanakambr*).

24. Johan Lange, *Primitive plantenavne og deres gruppering efter motiver* (Copenhagen, 1966), pp.93–94. "Horsehoof" is probably *Caltha palustris* (Lange, p.61), and "cockscomb" is probably *Rhinantus crista galli* (Olrik, 2:160 n.1). *Tagrør* 'reed' is *Phragmites communis*. See further, Johan Lange, *Ordbog over Danmarks plantenavne,* 3 vols. (Copenhagen: Ejnar Munksgaard, 1959–61), s.vv. "hestehov," "hanekam," and "tag" (together with its compounds).

25. A. Nordfelt, "Om det äldre Hamletproblemet: namnet och typen," in *Språkvetenskapliga sällskapets i Uppsala förhandlingar, 1925–1927*, 2:80–82.

26. Danish *rude* 'quadrangular plane' and *rude* 'rue' are assumed to be borrowed from Middle Low German; both probably go back to Latin *ruta* 'rue'. See Niels Åge Nielsen, *Dansk etymologisk ordbog*, 2d ed. (Copenhagen: Gyldendal, 1969), s.v. "rude."

27. The straw under which the eavesdropper hides himself ("submissusque stramento delituit") becomes in Belleforest's

retelling a quilt ("se cachant souz quelque loudier") and so in Shakespeare an arras. There can be no question that the original spy concealed himself under straw, whether it was floor straw or bed straw. Belleforest, writing nearly four centuries after Saxo, and in Paris, could not imagine royalty stepping on or sleeping upon mere straw and so rendered *stramentum* in its rare sense of "quilt" or "coverlet." But neither Saxo nor any of his Northern contemporaries would have found the bedroom straw unusual, and no Scandinavian translator or commentator has ever imagined that Saxo had in mind a blanket in this scene. The point needs to be emphasized because the rendering of *stramentum* as "quilt" has been accepted, without argument, by J. Dérocquigny, "Shakespeare et Belleforest," *Revue anglo-américaine* 6 (1923–24): 527–28, and by Gollancz, *Sources,* p.319, cited by Arthur P. Stabler, "The Sources of *Hamlet*: Some Corrections of the Record," *Research Studies* 32 (1964): 209 n. 6. The question is also raised by Marshall Blakemore Evans, *Der bestrafte Brudermord: sein Verhältnis zu Shakespeares Hamlet*, Theatergeschichtliche Forschungen 19 (Hamburg and Leipzig, 1910), p.18 n. 2.

28. The more elegant relative of this arrangement is no doubt the indoor facility familiar from European castles, in which the refuse passes from the hole in the seat to the moat or the ground below. For Scandinavian examples, see "Hemmelighed," in *Kulturhistorisk leksikon for nordisk middelalder* (Copenhagen: Rosenkilde & Bagger, 1961), 6:442–48.

29. Aarne-Thompson, Type 655. See further, Axel Olrik, "Märchen in Saxo Grammaticus," *Zeitschrift des Vereins für Volkskunde* 2 (1892): 119–23; F. von der Leyen, *Das Märchen in den Göttersagen der Edda* (Berlin: G. Reimer, 1899), pp.71–79, 85–86; and J. Schick, *Corpus Hamleticum* (Leipzig: Otto Harrassowitz, 1934–38), vols.4–5.

30. See Schick, *Corpus Hamleticum*, 4:384–429.

31. E. T. Kristensen, *Jyske Folkeminder* (Copenhagen: K. Schønberg, 1884), 7:no.20.

32. The point of the queen's first fault is that a freeborn woman had a covering or hood for her head, whereas a slave did

not, so that when it was cold the latter had to draw her cloak over her head. The second charge is connected with the fact that the gown of a wellborn woman reached to her ankles and was allowed its full length when she walked, whereas a bondmaid's clothing was girded high in order that she might more easily go about her tasks. As for the third, evidently only a thrallwoman was so vulgar as to consume what she had extracted from her teeth.

33. See A. P. Stabler, "Melancholy, Ambition, and Revenge in Belleforest's Hamlet," *PMLA* 81 (1966): 207–8; Werner Habicht, "Hamlets 'prophetisches Gemüt,'" *Fabula* 20(1979): 79–85.

34. *Grettis saga,* chap.22.

35. Otto Jiriczek, "Hamlet in Iran," *Zeitschrift des Vereins für Volkskunde* 10 (1900): 359. Detter, p.2, observes that the hero's sticks are employed symbolically both here and in the Brutus legend. For Brutus's gold-filled stick is a metaphor for himself, while Amleth's two sticks contain the wergild paid for his two companions and so correspond exactly to their worth. See Aarne-Thompson, Type 961B, for the best-known tale using the motif of money in the stick. The present incident in the *Vita Amlethi* probably draws on this folktale, in which a debtor returns to his creditor a gold-filled stick, apparently worthless, and then swears to him that he has repaid his debt. The tale is very old. It was known in ancient Greece: Konon *Narrations* 38; Stobaios *Florilegium* 3. 28. 21. See further, Joseph Fontenrose, *The Delphic Oracle* (Berkeley and Los Angeles: University of California Press, 1978), pp.118–19.

36. See, in general, Helen Engelstad, *Refil, Bunad, Tjeld* (Oslo: Gyldendal, 1952), pp.13–36. Notice that what is unusual about Amleth's strategy is not his plying his intended victims with drink and then burning them within the hall, which is an exceedingly common way of getting rid of one's enemies in Old Scandinavian stories: see the many citations in Inger Boberg, *Motif-Index of Early Icelandic Literature,* Bibliotheca Arnamagnaeana 27 (Copenhagen, 1966), K811.1 "Enemies invited to banquet (visit) and killed," and K812 "Victim burned in his own house." The unusual feature is rather the hero's use of the hangings and the crooks to render his many enemies helpless.

37. *Historia Langobardorum* 2. 28.

38. Peter Hallberg, *The Icelandic Saga*, trans. Paul Schach (Lincoln: University of Nebraska Press, 1962), p.107.

39. I observe in passing that the particular solution—the victory of King Viglek—is in harmony with Saxo's enthusiasm for a strong national monarch, though he also favors the ancient right of the people to choose their own king. On Saxo's views in this regard, see Kurt Johannesson, *Saxo Grammaticus: komposition och världsbild i "Gesta Danorum"* (Stockholm: Almqvist & Wiksell, 1978), pp.315–21.

40. Like foster brotherhood, sworn brotherhood (or blood brotherhood) is a variety of fictive brotherhood frequently mentioned in Northern literature. The ritual that solemnized sworn brotherhood, including the oath of avenging the other's death like a brother, is described in *Gísla saga,* chap.6, and *Fóstbræðra saga*, chap.2. Old Icelandic *fóstbróðir* means both "sworn brother" and "foster brother."

41. The reuse of the trick results in Amleth's having two wives, though his British spouse is not mentioned again after the return to Denmark. Multiple marriages did in fact take place occasionally in the North (Herrmann, 2:290; Fisher & Davidson, 2:65–66). Olrik, 2:174–77, believes that since the motif of double marriage was somewhat fashionable in twelfth-century European literature, its appearance in the Hamlet story is due to its popularity with some storyteller. Johannesson, *Saxo Grammaticus*, p.127, makes the interesting suggestion that Amleth's taking a second wife is an expression of the lack of *temperantia*, or moderation, shown by the hero in the continuation. His *intemperantia* begins with his men's fancy attire and his own illustrated shield and luxuriously outfitted ships; it continues with his acquiring a second wife; and it ends with his attack on Viglek, which leads to his downfall. The hero's earlier self-denial is followed by a self-indulgence which is at first reasonable but becomes gradually excessive.

42. Aarne-Thompson, Type 930. See also Olrik, 2:170–77; J. Schick, *Corpus Hamleticum,* vols. 1, 2.

43. The mysterious Undensakre is perhaps connected with the Icelandic *Ódáinsakr* 'Undeath Field'. See Herrmann, 2:252–53, 293–94; de Vries, *Altgermanische Religionsgeschichte,* 2:285.

44. E. T. Kristensen, *Jyske folkeminder* (Kolding: Konrad Jørgensen, 1886), 8:no.152

45. For a detailed discussion of Viglek and of the traditions in which he figures outside of Saxo's story, see Niels Lukman, "British and Danish Traditions," *Classica et Mediaevalia* 6 (1944): 74–82.

46. Inger M. Boberg, "Saxo's Hamlet," *American-Scandinavian Review* 44 (March 1956): 53.

47. In this paragraph I draw in part on Professor Niels Lukman's unpublished notes, "Hamlet og Amleth," dated Copenhagen, 1945, to which the author kindly gave me access.

48. Petrus Erasmus Müller and Joannes Matthias Velschow, eds., *Saxonis Grammatici Historia Danica,* 2:133.

49. "AMLED — YPPERSTE / OLDTIDS — SNILLE / TEED SIG TAABE / TIL HÆVNENS TIME — / KAARET PAA TING / AF JYDER TIL KONGE / HØJSAT HAN HVILER / PAA AMMELHEDE — . Amleth, who probably never lived, is the most buried personage in Denmark. His remains lie in some two dozen different sites. Nearly all of these are in Jutland, where the many place-names beginning with Am- together with the familiarity of Saxo's story have suggested to local etymologists that this or that village was the spot to which Saxo refers. On these places, see Olrik, 2:159–60; Thøger Larsen, "Amlet og hans grav," *Atlantis* 2 (1924): 564–75; O. Løye, *Hamlets grav i Ammelhede ved Randers* (Randers: Propaganda Komiteen for Randers By og Havn, 1933), or his popular article, "The Historical Hamlet and His Grave," *American-Scandinavian Review* 21 (1933): 201–7; Niels Lukman, "'Hamlets Grave' i Jylland," *Helsingør dagblad*, March 15, 1945; and Harry Ludvigsen, "Nyt liv i den gamle Hamlet," *Jyllands-posten* (December 2, 1975). According to George P. Hansen, *The Legend of Hamlet*; (1887: reprint ed., New York: AMS Press, 1972), pp.13–14, there was even a barrow

of Amleth on the island of Fyn. On Hamlet's grave at Elsinore, see, especially, Laurits Pedersen, *Kronborg have* (Copenhagen: G. E. C. Gad, 1920), pp.136–42.

Appendix I

1. Ellen Jørgensen, *Annales Danici medii aevi* (Copenhagen: G. E. C. Gad, 1920), pp.64 (*Annales Ryenses),* 132 *(Annales Slesvicenses).* M. Lorenzen, *Gammeldanske krøniker* (Copenhagen: S. L. Møller, 1887–1913), pp.222–23 *(Runekrøniken,* 16–19 (*Gesta Danorum pa danskæ*), 204–5 (*Sagnkrøniken i Stockholm*). On the texts see, especially, Ellen Jørgensen, *Middelalderlig historisk litteratur paa modersmaalet* (Copenhagen: J. Jørgensen, 1930).

2. Lorenzen, *Gammeldanske krøniker,* p.17.

Appendix II

1. M. Mackeprang and Sigrid Flamand Christensen, *Kronborgtapeterne* (Copenhagen: A.F. Høst, 1950), pp.5–6. Antonius Samfleth painted the likeness of 117 Danish kings in 1574, and there was said to be a manuscript with paintings of all the kings of Demark belonging to Henrik Rantzau.

2. *Historia de omnibus Gothorum Sueonumque regibus,* 1554.

3. Mackeprang and Christensen, *Kronborgtapeterne,* pp.4–5.

4. *The Danish Rhyme Chronicle* was a verse chronicle composed at Sorø Monastery on Zealand. It was the first Danish book to be printed (1495). In it each Danish monarch, speaking in rhymed couplets, addresses the reader and relates his story in his own words. Following the tradition of *The Annals of Ryd* the chronicle includes Ørvendil, Fengi, and Amleth as kings of Denmark. The two brothers each offer in turn a six-verse account of their reigns, and then Amelth steps forth to deliver the

longest and liveliest speech in the whole poem. See Helge Toldberg, ed., *Den danske rimkrønike*, 3 vols. (Copenhagen: J. H. Schultz, 1958–61). The verses concerning Amleth are found in 1:18–28; they are translated into French in Alexandre Büchner, *Hamlet le Danois*, pp.85–93.

5. Mackeprang and Christensen, *Kronborgtapeterne*, pp.66–78.

6. Thott 797. Amblett is a copy of Dan II or Dan III in Thott 795. Both manuscripts are in the Royal Library, Copenhagen.

7. Codex Holm K 49, dated 1597, is in the Royal Library, Stockholm.

8. Gl. kgl. Saml. 813 (fig.43) may have belonged to King Christian IV, who died in 1648. A copy of it was made in 1638 (the copy is Ny kgl. Saml. 586, and Thott 796 is a copy of one of the two). Gl. kgl. Saml. 815 (fig.4) is dated 1658, and has a German prose text. These manuscripts are in the Royal Library, Copenhagen. For illustrations relating to Shakespeare's *Hamlet*, see Raymond Mander and Joe Mitchenson, comps., and Herbert Marshall, ed., *Hamlet through the Ages: A Pictorial Record from 1709* (London: Rockliff Publ. Corp., 1952).

Selected Bibliography

Useful Editions of Saxo

Müller, Petrus Erasmus, and Velschow, Joannes Matthias, eds. *Saxonis Grammatici Historia Danica*. 2 vols. Copenhagen: Gyldendal, 1839–58.

Olrik, Jørgen and Ræder, Hans, eds. *Saxonis Gesta Danorum*. 2 vols. Copenhagen: Munksgaard, 1931–57.

Stephanius, Stephanus Iohannis, ed. *Saxonis Grammatici Historiae Danicae libri XVI*. 2 vols. Sorø: Ioachimus Moltkenius, 1644–45.

English Translations of Saxo

Elton, Oliver, trans., and Powell, Frederick York. *The First Nine Books of the Danish History of Saxo Grammaticus: With Some Considerations on Saxo's Sources, Historical Methods, and Folk-Lore*. Publications of the Folk-Lore Society, no.33 (1893). Reprint ed., Nendeln, Liechtenstein: Kraus Reprint Limited, 1967.

Fisher, Peter, trans., and Davidson, Hilda Ellis, ed. *Saxo Grammaticus: The History of the Danes*. 2 vols. Cambridge: D. S. Brewer; Totowa, N.J: Rowman & Littlefield, 1979–80.

A Selection of Critical Works concerning the Hamlet of Tradition

Amory, Frederic. "The Medieval Hamlet: A Lesson in the Use and Abuse of a Myth." *Deutsche Vierteljahrsschrift für Literaturwissenschaft und Geistesgeschichte* 51 (1977): 357–95.

Anderson, Florence M. B. "The Insanity of the Hero—An Intrinsic Detail of the Orestes Vendetta." *TAPA* 58 (1927): 43–62.

Boberg, Inger Margrethe. "Saxo's Hamlet." *American-Scandinavian Review* 44 (March 1956): 50–56.

Detter, Ferd. "Die Hamletsage." *ZfdA* 36 (1892): 1–25.

Dumézil, Georges. "Horwendillus." In *From Myth to Fiction*, translated by Derek Coltman, pp. 193–201. Chicago and London: University of Chicago Press, 1973.

Elton, Oliver. "Saxo's Hamlet." In *The First Nine Books of the Danish History of Saxo Grammaticus . . .*, edited by Oliver Elton and Federick York Powell, pp. 398–413. Publications of the Folk-Lore Society, no. 33 (1893). Reprint ed., Nendeln, Liechtenstein: Kraus Reprint Limited, 1967.

Fisher, Peter, trans., and Davidson, Hilda Ellis, ed. *Saxo Grammaticus: The History of the Danes*. 2 vols. Cambridge: D. S. Brewer; Totowa, N.J: Rowman and Littlefield, 1979–80.

Gollancz, Israel, ed. and trans. *Hamlet in Iceland: Being the Icelandic Romantic Ambales Saga, with Extracts from Five Ambales Rimur and Other Illustrative Texts, for the Most Part Now First Printed, and an Introductory Essay*. Northern Library, vol. 3. London: David Nutt, 1898

———. *The Sources of Hamlet, with an Essay on the Legend. London,* 1926. Reprint ed., London: Frank Cass & Co., 1967.

Herrmann, Paul. *Erläuterungen zu den ersten neun Büchern der Dänischen Geschichte des Saxo Grammaticus*. 2 vols. Leipzig: Wilhelm Engelmann, 1901–22.

Heusler, Andreas. "Amlethus." In *Reallexikon der Germanischen Altertumskunde*, ed. Johannes Hoops, 1:78–79. Strassburg: K. J. Trübner, 1911–13.

Jiriczek, Otto L. "Die Amlethsage auf Island." In *Beiträge zur Volkskunde: Festschrift für Karl Weinhold, Germanistische Abhandlungen* 12 (Breslau, 1896): 59–108.

______. "Hamlet in Iran." *Zeitschrift des Vereins für Volkskunde* 10 (1900): 353–364.

Krause, Wolfgang. "Die Hamletstrophe Snæbjǫrns." In *Festschrift für Konstantin Reichardt*, edited by Christian Gellinek, pp.87–97. Bern: A. Francke, 1969.

Kuhn, H. "Amled." In *Reallexikon der germanischen Altertumskunde,* by Johannes Hoops, edited by Heinrich Beck et al., 1:253. 2d ed. Berlin and New York: Walter de Gruyter, 1973

Lukman, Niels. "British and Danish Traditions: Some Contacts and Relations." *Classica et Mediaevalia* 6 (1944): 72–109.

______. "Hamlet og Amleth." Copenhagen, 1945. Manuscript.

Meissner, R. "Der Name Hamlet." *Indogermanische Forschungen* 45 (1927): 370–94.

Murray, Gilbert. *Hamlet and Orestes: A Study in Traditional Types.* New York: Oxford University Press, 1914.

Nordfelt, A. "Om det äldre Hamletsproblemet: namnet och typen." In *Språkvetenskapliga sällskapets i Uppsala Förhandlingar 1925–1927, Uppsala Universitets årsskrift* 1927, 2:55–94. Uppsala, 1927.

Olrik, Axel. "Amledsagnet på island." *Arkiv för nordisk filologi* 15 (1899): 360–76.

______. "Danmarks Heltedigtning V." Notes in the Danish Folklore Archives.

______. "Märchen in Saxo Grammaticus." *Zeitschrift des Vereins für Volkskunde* 2 (1892): 117–23.

______. *Kilderne til Sakses oldhistorie: en literaturhistorisk undersøgelse.* 2 vols. Copenhagen: G. E. C. Gad, 1894.

Olrik, Jørgen. "'Avnebag': forklaring til en gaade i Amled-sagnet."

In *Festskrift til H. F. Feilberg, fra nordiske sprog- og folkemindeforskere,* pp.98–100. Stockholm, Copenhagen, Kristiania: P. A. Norstedt & Söner et al., 1911.

Schick, Josef. *Corpus Hamleticum: Hamlet in Sage und Dichtung, Kunst und Musik.* 4 vols. (vols. 1, 2, 4, 5). Berlin: Emil Felber; Leipzig: Otto Harrasowitz, 1912–38.

Schneider, Hermann. *Nordgermanische Heldensage.* Berlin and Leipzig: Walter de Gruyter, 1933.

Setälä, E. N. "Kullervo-Hamlet: Ein sagenvergleichender Versuch." *Finnisch-Ugrische Forschungen* 3 (1903): 61–97; 7 (1907): 188–264; 10 (1910): 44–127.

Sperber, Hans. "The Conundrums in Saxo's Hamlet Episode." *PMLA* 64 (1949): 864–70.

Zenker, Rudolf. *Boeve-Amlethus: Das altfranzösische Epos von Boeve de Hamtone und der Ursprung der Hamletsage. Literarhistorische Forschungen,* vol. 32. Berlin and Leipzig, 1904.

A Selection of Works concerning Belleforest's and Shakespeare's Hamlet

Büchner, Alexandre. *Hamlet le Danois.* Paris: Librairie Hachette and Cie., 1878.

Bullough, Geoffrey, ed. *Narrative and Dramatic Sources of Shakespeare.* vol. 7. London: Routledge and Kegan Paul, 1973.

Conklin, Paul S. *A History of "Hamlet" Criticism, 1601–1821.* New York: Humanities Press, 1957.

Dollerup, Cay. *Denmark, "Hamlet," and Shakespeare: A Study of Englishmen's Knowledge of Denmark towards the End of the Sixteenth Century with Special Reference to "Hamlet."* 2 vols. Salzburg Studies in English Literature. Salzburg: Institut für englische Sprache und Literatur, Universität Salzburg, 1975.

Gollancz, Israel. *The Sources of Hamlet, with an Essay on the Legend.* London, 1926. Reprint ed., London: Frank Cass & Co., 1967

Gottschalk, Paul, *The Meanings of Hamlet: Modes of Literary Interpretation since Bradley*. Albuquerque: University of New Mexico Press, 1972.

Henriques, Alf. *Shakespeare og Danmark indtil* 1840. Copenhagen: E. Munksgaard, 1941.

______. "Shakespeare and Denmark: 1900–1949." *Shakespeare Survey* 3 (1950): 107–15.

Honigman, E. A. J. "The Date of *Hamlet*." *Shakespeare Survey* 9 (1956): 24–34.

Jenkins, Harold. "'Hamlet' Then till Now." *Shakespeare Survey* 18 (1965): 34–45.

Jones, Ernest. *Hamlet and Oedipus*. 1949; reprint ed., Garden City, N.Y: Doubleday & Co., Anchor Books, 1954.

Krappe, Alexander H. "Shakespeare in Romance Folk-Lore." *Neuphilologische Mitteilungen* 27 (1926): 65–76.

Law, Robert Adger. "Belleforest, Shakespeare, and Kyd." In *Joseph Quincy Adams Memorial Studies*, edited by James G. McManaway, Giles E. Dawson, and Edwin E. Willoughby, pp.279–94. Washington: Folger Shakespeare Library, 1948.

Leech, Clifford, "Studies in *Hamlet:* 1901–1955." *Shakespeare Survey* 9 (1956): 1–15.

Muir, Kenneth. *Shakespeare's Sources*. Vol. 1. London: Methuen, 1961.

Schulze, F. W. "François Belleforests Histoire Tragique d'Amleth." In *Im Dienste der Sprache: Festschrift für Victor Klemperer,* edited by Horst Heintz and Erwin Silzer, pp.362–74. Halle: M. Niemeyer, 1958.

Stabler, Arthur P. "Elective Monarchy in the Sources of *Hamlet*." *Studies in Philology* 62 (1965): 654–61.

______. "King Hamlet's Ghost in Belleforest?" *PMLA* 77 (1962): 18–20.

______. "Melancholy, Ambition, and Revenge in Belleforest's Hamlet." *PMLA* 81 (1966): 207–13.

______. "More on the Search for Yorick's Skull; or, The Goths Refuted." *Shakespeare Studies* 7 (1974): 203–8.

______. "The Sources of the German Hamlet." *Shakespeare Studies* 5 (1969): 97-105

______. "The Sources of *Hamlet*: Some Corrections of the Record." *Research Studies* 32 (1964): 207–16.
Weitz, Morris. *Hamlet and the Philosophy of Literary Criticism.* Chicago and London: University of Chicago Press, 1964.
Whitaker, Virgil K. *Shakespeare's Use of Learning*. San Marino, Calif: Huntington Library, 1953.

Index